DIVIDED LOYALTIES

DIVIDED LOYALTIES

The Diary of a Basketball Father

BOB HURLEY, SR.
WITH
PHIL PEPE

With Forewords by
Mike Krzyzewski and P.J. Carlesimo

ZEBRA BOOKS
A KENSINGTON CORPORATION

ZEBRA BOOKS are published by

Kensington Publishing Corp.
475 Park Avenue South
New York, NY 10016

First Printing: November, 1993

Printed in the United States of America

ISBN   0-8217-4391-0

To Sean Hurley, our "other" son, who we had for only 10 days. I am certain you would have made us just as proud of you as Bobby, Danny, and Melissa have.
And to my dad, Robert Hurley, Sr., and Chris's dad, Steven Ledzion. You are never out of our thoughts.

ACKNOWLEDGMENTS

So many people helped with the preparation of this book, with their support, their encouragement and their involvement with St. Anthony. The authors wish to thank the following:

All those who played basketball and helped foster the St. Anthony tradition over the past 21 years, especially the 1992–93 championship team.

All the assistant coaches who helped mold, develop, and guide a long list of champions, especially the current staff of George Canda, Tom Cusick, Jim Morley, Hassan Abdullah, Greg Hall, and Gary Pitchford.

Sister Mary Felicia, principal of St. Anthony, and Sister Mary Alan, St. Anthony Athletic Director. Also Sister Diane, Margie Calabrese, Fran Kochanski and C.J. Flaherty and Barbara Daus of St. Anthony.

Faithful and loyal friends, Bob (Mousey) Hahner, Cong. Frank Guarini, Bob Sears, Harry Traina, John Cichetti, Ron Olzowy, Eddie (The Faa) Ford, Tom Olivieri, Marty Nielon, Mary Costello, Kevin Callahan, Jack Moore and Artie Zinicola, Brian Doherty and Rich McKeever of Artie's Restaurant.

Special thanks to Jerry Cuicci, who generously provided most of the photographs used in this book. Although he is not a professional photographer, he freely gave of his time to record on film most of the important events for St. Anthony basketball and the Hurleys.

Our thanks, also, to Walter Zacharius of Zebra Books for his vision, to Wally Exman, for his encouragement and expertise, to Matt Merola and to Basil Kane.

B.H.
P.P.

CONTENTS

FOREWORD

by MIKE KRZYZEWSKI
Head Coach, Basketball
Duke University

I have had the opportunity to watch the teams of Bob Hurley, Sr., play for many years. They played with great intensity, uncommon teamwork, and they usually won!

Everything seemed to start on the defensive end of the court for his teams. The kids would throw themselves into a teamlike identity and do anything they could to stop their opponents. I have always felt that the sign of a good coach really is in direct proportion to how hard his team would play. In this case, Bob Hurley, Sr., is at the highest level of coaching.

Six years ago, I began a very close relationship with the Hurley family. It was then that I started recruiting Bob's son, Bobby, to play for me here at Duke University. During those six years I found that Bob Hurley, Sr., and his family—Mrs. Hurley, Chris; sons Bobby and Danny; daughter Melissa—are very special people. They are totally committed to the development of the youngsters who play for St. Anthony. As hard as Bob works in making his kids better basketball players, he equals that effort with what he does for them off the court. He truly loves his players and helps them in every way that he can.

In coaching his son, Bobby, I found that Bobby possessed special traits. Sure, he was an outstanding player, but Bobby also brought unusual qualities to our basketball team. His daring and his amazing will to win helped us immensely in winning two national championships. Bobby learned his unusual qualities from his father. His total commitment to work and to his team has made him one of the most storied players in the history of college basketball.

After spending four years with Bobby, I feel I know even more now what Bob, Sr., has done for his youngsters over the years. He has helped to make them all winners. I guess that is the best word I can use to describe Bob Hurley, Sr. He is a winner!

I hope that after reading more about him, your admiration for him will be as high as mine.

FOREWORD

By P.J. CARLESIMO
Head Basketball Coach
Seton Hall University

Bob Hurley's accomplishments at St. Anthony High School are truly remarkable. His players reflect the knowledge and discipline that have long been the trademark of his program. Bob is one of the outstanding teachers of basketball, and his players graduate with a real understanding of the game.

Terry Dehere, Jerry Walker, and Danny Hurley brought the same level of excellence to our program at Seton Hall. There have been many outstanding basketball players at St. Anthony, but the coaching defines the program.

PREFACE

I first met Bob Hurley, Sr., in the summer of 1992, at the basketball camp he runs for youngsters at a New Jersey high school.

I had, of course, read about him and heard about him; about the uniquely successfuly basketball program he runs at St. Anthony High School in Jersey City; about his own sons, Bobby and Danny, and the dozens of players he has coached who have gone on to have successful college careers. And I had formed some preconceptions about Bob Hurley, Sr.

I assumed he combed New York and New Jersey, scounting and proselytizing grammar school basketball players. I figured he culled the best of the best, then wooed them to St. Anthony with scholarships and promises of college glory and, eventually, the prospect of NBA gold. I pictured him a slave-driving, whip-cracking martinet at practice, a referee-baiting, player-abusing intimidator on the sidelines during games. I imagined his players to be a collection of toughs, filled with a sense of self-importance, impertinence to strangers and defiance of society.

I was wrong. Oh, boy, was I wrong. On all counts.

The many stories I had heard that helped me form these pre-conceptions I can now only attribute to sour grapes and envy.

For Bob Hurley has engendered sour grapes from many of the coaches he has brought to their knees in defeat; he has fostered envy by virtue of an incredible, almost unbelievable string of suc-cesses—16 Parochial B New Jersey State championships, four ap-pearances in the final game and three championships in the five years of the statewide Tournament of Champions, an un-defeated season and the mythical national high school cham-pionship in 1989, and a coaching record of 547–61, which computes to an amazing winning percentage of .89967.

But what he has accomplished on the basketball court tells only in small part the story of Bob Hurley, Sr., for he is much more than just a basketball coach.

He is a devoted family man, a pillar of the community, a man who believes in giving something back to the sport he loves and to the place where he was born, raised and still lives. As a Senior Probation Officer in Hudson County, he has worked tirelessly to help fight the insidious scourge of drug abuse that plagues this nation's inner cities.

Yet, it is his work, and his singular success, on and off the court, as basketball coach of St. Anthony that sets him apart, not just through his sons, but with dozens of others who have been coached by him, and touched by him. Such as Jerry Walker of Seton Hall.

"Mr. Hurley taught me more than how to play basketball," Walker said. "He taught me about life."

For many of the youngsters of St. Anthony, basketball is life, and life is basketball. They have learned the value of competition and the virtue of hard work, dedication, and self-sacrifice; they have learned that there is a way out of the inner city and there are rewards for honest effort.

For Bob Hurley, Sr., his reward is in channeling youngsters

away from the streets, helping them mature as basketball players and young men, sending them off to college and watching them become successful people.

He could have parlayed his success into personal gain. He could have abandoned Jersey City, the dingy gyms of high school basketball, and opted for the glory, fame, and fortune of big-time college basketball. He has had many opportunities to do so, but he has chosen to remain in Jersey City, at St. Anthony. For that choice, he has gained the respect, gratitude, and unstinting loyalty of hundreds of St. Anthony alumni and friends.

To understand who and what Bob Hurley, Sr., is, one must witness his St. Anthony team as I did. Not only on the court, but off the court.

Off the court, they are courteous, well mannered, and well groomed. They arrive at the gym in a group, neatly dressed in their marooon and gold St. Anthony sweaters. They sit quietly in the stands until it is time to repair to their dressing room to get ready to perform.

On the court, they play with a clocklike precision, with a fierce determination, with unmatched skill and uncommon (for teenagers) selflessness. They are a team in every sense of the word. There are no stars, no egos on the St. Anthony team.

It has been said that any high school youngster can play offense. He can shoot and dribble, run and jump. Getting him to play defense is another matter. Offense is fun. Defense is work. The St. Anthony team excels on defense. They are tenacious. They are relentless. They are dedicated. The energy the St. Anthony players expend on defense speaks volumes of Bob Hurley, Sr., as a coach, a motivator, a disciplinarian.

What follows is a diary of one basketball season, the 1992–93 season, as Bob Hurley, Sr., divides his attention, and his loyalties, monitoring the fortune of three basketball teams—his own St. Anthony team, his son Bobby's Duke team, and his son Danny's Seton Hall team.

· PREFACE ·

The words belong to Bob Hurley, Sr. However, to properly capture the emotion and importance of some situations, Bob wanted to include the voices of his wife, Chris, Bob Jr., and Danny, thus making this book in certain respects a family diary as well.

Here, then, is a microcosm of the basketball life of Bob Hurley, Sr., just one year in what has been a 21-year career as coach at St. Anthony, and what, if he has his way, will continue for at least another 21 years of winning, on and off the basketball court.

Phil Pepe
Englewood, N.J.
May 1993

The City of Brotherly Love: March 26, 1992

I couldn't begin to estimate how many basketball games I've played, coached, and seen. Let's see. I've coached more than 600, played in a couple of hundred, and seen a few hundred more. Throw in pickup games, games I've watched on TV, games in summer leagues, scrimmages and games in the summer camp I run in New Jersey, and it's probably a couple of thousand.

Two thousand basketball games and I don't ever remember being as nervous as I was in the Philadelphia Spectrum on the night of March 26, 1992.

On that night, Duke was playing Seton Hall in the NCAA East Regional semifinal, what has come to be known as the "Sweet Sixteen," the last 16 teams remaining of the original NCAA championship tournament field of 64 in what the media refers to as "March Madness."

To everybody else, the matchup was Duke vs. Seton Hall. To us Hurleys, it was Bobby against Danny. My two sons going head-to-head, and don't think that wasn't nerve-racking for a father.

As I look back at it now, it was a wonderful thing, something a father could be proud of. But to my wife, Chris, and me, it was torture.

The press had made a big thing of it. Brothers playing against each other in the NCAA quarterfinals. It had never happened before, so it was a big story all over the country. The writers and television broadcasters ate it up and milked it for all it was worth. To a fan, I suppose it was interesting. To a parent, it was pure agony.

I felt for Bobby. He was an all-American, the point guard and floor leader for Duke, which was trying to become the first team in almost 20 years to win back-to-back NCAA championships. Because of the position he plays, if he had a bad game, it could mean a loss for Duke.

So, Bobby was in a no-win situation playing against his younger brother. If he had a good game and Duke won, everybody would say it figured because he's supposed to be a better player than his brother, older and more experienced. If he had a bad game and Duke lost, it would be all Bobby's fault.

• • •

Bobby Hurley: As difficult as it was on Danny and me, it had to be tougher on my parents. Especially my mom. You could tell by looking at her face that she was under a lot of stress.

• • •

Then I thought of Danny, and something he had said before the game.

• • •

Danny Hurley: Not only was I playing against a kid who's a first team all-American, he's my older brother. So what kind of situation am I in? He's the all-American, I'm the younger brother. I'm on the bench at Seton Hall, and I'm going to be

2

playing more in that game than I normally do because the coach thinks it's going to affect the way Bobby plays.

. . .

As a father, I didn't like the strategy of Seton Hall coach P.J. Carlesimo to put Danny on Bobby. As a coach, I understood what P.J. was doing. He figured anything he could do to take Bobby out of his game would give Seton Hall a better chance to win. In his position, I would have done the same thing.

But I wasn't in PJ's position. I was in the position of being a father watching his two sons playing against each other and not being able to root for either of them.

Some people said I should have been rooting for Duke because they were trying to do something that hadn't been done in 20 years, and because Bobby was a junior and Danny was only a freshman, and he'd get other chances.

That crossed my mind, but I couldn't root for Duke because Terry Dehere and Jerry Walker played for Seton Hall, too, and they wouldn't allow me to root for Duke. Terry and Jerry both played for me at St. Anthony and I was reminded of the fact that they're close to me and, like Bobby, they also were juniors.

I really like those kids, Terry and Jerry, a great deal. But I love my sons. It's like Al McGuire once said when he was coaching at Marquette and his son was playing for him and somebody was competing with his son for a job.

"If you're just as good as my son," Al said, "you're in trouble, because he's my son."

. . .

Danny: It was a media event, the biggest thing I've ever been involved in. My parents were torn. They wanted Bobby to win and they wanted me to win. They didn't know how to root. They were in limbo, I guess.

. . .

So here I was, just watching the game, not rooting, my mind going back and forth and my insides churning. I couldn't afford to root for either team, so I didn't. Chris solved the problem for herself by cheering for anything good that related to St. Anthony. If Bobby did something good, she cheered. If Danny, Terry, or Jerry did something good, she cheered. She just kept jumping up and down and it was weird because we were sitting in the Duke section and people couldn't figure out what she was doing.

I just sat there. I knew it was going to be a disaster, and it was.

Bobby and Danny are more than just brothers, they're buddies. They're very close. They're only 18 months apart and they do everything together.

I had my eyes on both of them as they warmed up before the game. They seemed amused by the situation. When they got close to each other, I could see them stealing glances at each other and they both would look like they were about to break out laughing. And I was dying inside.

. . .

Danny: In warmups, we were looking at each other and laughing. It was like a big joke to us.

. . .

It's not that they weren't going to take the game seriously. As close as they are and as well as they get along, both Bobby and Danny are very competitive, especially against each other. It's no different than it is with any siblings.

In the summer, when they come to my basketball camp or get together in the playgrounds and gyms, I never let them play on the same team or guard each other because of their competitiveness. Invariably, they would get into a dispute.

4

. . .

Danny: When we were little, we were real competitive and we could never play with each other or against each other. We'd just start fighting. If I thought he wasn't passing me the ball because he's my brother, I'd get mad and yell at him, and he would do the same thing. But as we got older, we got closer. Now, we're real close.

. . .

During the season, Danny was not playing as much as he would have liked at Seton Hall, and Bobby often called him and talked to him, trying to lift his spirits and telling him to hang in there, his time would come.

Little did Bobby know Danny's time would come this night in Philadelphia, against him. Danny played 18 minutes that night, more than he usually played. I knew Bobby was not going to be the player he normally was. As much as he wanted to win, I knew he didn't want to have a good game at the expense of his brother.

. . .

Bobby: It was difficult to concentrate. I couldn't really play as intense as I normally do because I was going up against Danny. I think that really affected me.

. . .

Bobby scored only four points in that game, well below his average, and he committed six turnovers, which is very uncharacteristic of him. Danny, who had his own problems, took four shots and missed them all and scored no points. He did succeed in taking Bobby out of his game, but Duke had too many weapons and beat Seton Hall, 81—69.

That was one game I couldn't enjoy and I was glad when it

was over. With Seton Hall eliminated, I could afford the luxury of rooting again. Now I was a Duke fan. Two nights later, Duke beat Kentucky in the East Regional championship on a miraculous shot by Christian Laettner, that memorable turnaround jumper at the buzzer. And we were off to Minneapolis for the Final Four.

Duke played Indiana in the semis and it was obvious from the start that Indiana coach Bobby Knight's strategy was to stop Laettner by ganging up on him, double and triple teaming him. The strategy worked. Laettner had more turnovers than points in the first half, but Bobby kept Duke in the game with sixteen points, including four 3s.

Indiana led at the half by five, but Laettner got his game together in the second half and Duke won. Bobby finished with 26 points, a career high, and six 3s and Duke was matched against Michigan's Fab Five, a starting team made up entirely of freshmen, in the championship game.

Once again, Duke trailed at halftime, but only by a point, and once again they turned it on in the second half to win by 20 and become the first team since 1973 to win back-to-back NCAA championships. Bobby was voted the Most Valuable Player of the tournament, although he scored only nine points in the championship game, but he did have seven assists.

But Bobby's game never has been about points, something Duke Coach Mike Krzyzewski appreciates.

"He missed some shots," Coach K said after the game, "but how he took them was important. He took them aggressively, and his teammates said, 'That kid wants to win.' For what we want, there's nobody who's been any better than Bobby."

Bobby's game always has been about winning. As long as he's been involved in games, he's been involved in winning, and helping Duke win its second consecutive national championship had put an exclamation mark to what had been for him a fabulous year.

Naturally, we were all excited and happy for Bobby, but the lasting memory of the season, and not necessarily a completely pleasant one, would be the East Regional semifinal, Duke against Seton Hall, Bobby against Danny. People have asked me if I would want to go through that again, with all the nervousness, all the agony, all the mixed emotions. Could I stand it a second time?

To tell you the truth, despite the agony, I was hoping to have to go through that one more time. Duke vs. Seton Hall in the 1993 NCAA final; Bobby against Danny; my two sons going against each other one more time for the national championship. I could live with that.

Friday, November 27

Now it begins. It's the first day of practice for my St. Anthony team, a day that, for me, is always filled with hope, anticipation, excitement, and mystery. The official start of a new season. A new beginning.

In high school basketball, you never know what to expect. The kids are so young, there's such a great turnover from one season to the next, and often a great difference in a teenager from his junior year to his senior year, from being 16 years old to turning 17. Kids can mature quickly at that age. They can grow several inches over the summer, get bigger and stronger and, because most of them have been playing in leagues and in playgrounds all summer, they can improve quite a bit.

As I start this new season, I really don't know how good we can be. I have an idea of our potential, but you never can be sure.

The college season has already begun, but Duke still has not played its first game and I know Bobby must be anxious to get going, even though he had a busy summer. He was invited to join the college all-stars who played against the "Dream Team," helping them get ready for the Olympics. They played in California and in Monaco, which was a great experience for them. Not only did they get to see some of the world, they got a chance to play against the best players in the game.

Bobby did very well and more than held his own against Magic Johnson, Michael Jordan, and the rest. All the reports we got and everything we read in the papers and magazines indicated Bobby was the outstanding player among the All-Stars. There were a lot of nice things said about him by people who witnessed the scrimmages, which were closed to the press and public.

Magic: "He's about as good as anybody I've seen playing college ball. Whew! He can dribble. He would be a starter on most teams if he was in the league now."

Jordan: "He surprised me. I thought he'd be average, but his penetration is unbelievable."

Charles Barkley: "He's a great player."

Chuck Daly, coach of the U.S. team: "I was shocked. It's the Mark Price look. It's the John Stockton look. You don't expect him to be as good as he is. We just couldn't handle him. He's the total package."

Lenny Wilkens, who coaches the Cleveland Cavaliers and was an assistant to Daly with the Dream Team and was an outstanding NBA guard himself, was asked if he thought Bobby would be effective in the NBA. "Hell, yes," Wilkins said. "He just looks out of place."

Because of his size, a shade over six feet, 165 pounds, some people had expressed doubts about Bobby as an NBA player. But he put a lot of those doubts to rest during the summer against the Dream Team. I know reading all those comments made Bobby feel good. What didn't make him feel so good was Duke being rated No. 4 in the preseason national rankings, although they were coming off two consecutive national championships

10

and the only players they lost were Christian Laettner and Brian Davis.

I've never seen Bobby so focused. It's probably because he's going into his senior year and perhaps because of the lack of respect for Duke this time around. It's also nearing the end of some personal goals, such as the all-time NCAA record for assists, the possibility of playing in another championship game and playing with the pros.

I was just as pleased that Duke was rated no higher than fourth. It would give them some incentive, something to shoot for, a challenge. Bobby is the kind of young man who responds well to a challenge. He has all his life.

Seton Hall got off to a good start, finishing second to Indiana in the preseason National Invitation Tournament. Danny got a chance to play quite a bit and he played well, so right now he's a happy camper. But it's still a long season, a long way to March Madness.

Now, here in the Seton Hall gym in South Orange, my immediate concern was getting the St. Anthony team, the Friars, ready for the season, which would begin before we knew it.

I'm starting my 26th year at St. Anthony, my 21st as head coach, and I still have the same exhilaration, the same anxiety, the same excitement I had in my first year. I still love the challenge. I love the expectation. I love seeing kids develop and improve and succeed. There isn't anything I'd rather be doing at this time of year. I'm a basketball guy. I love it.

I'm also a lifelong Jersey City guy. I was born in Jersey City, grew up in Jersey City, went to school in Jersey City, work in Jersey City, and still live in Jersey City. Chris is a lifelong Jersey City girl. I met her when we were kids. She lived in Sacred Heart parish, the parish next to mine, and both of us have lived our entire lives within a 20-block radius of where we were born.

We're uncomplicated people, our main interests being our family and basketball. We live in a modest home in the Greenville section of Jersey City, a predominantly Irish—American and Italian—American neighborhood with rows of attached and se-miattached two-bedroom homes, about a 15-minute drive from St. Anthony. We thought about buying a small summer home in the Poconos once, but then we realized we'd never use it.

I was named after my father, Robert Patrick Hurley, so I actually am a junior. My son Bobby is not. He's Robert Matthew. But since we're both involved in basketball, it makes it easier for people to call us Bob Senior and Bobby Junior.

My dad, who passed away 10 years ago, was with the Jersey City Police Department for more than 40 years, first as an officer, then as a detective. He was a semipro baseball pitcher, good enough that he might have had a career as a pro. But he went off to World War II and when he returned, he was too old.

When I was a kid, Dad would take me to the park after dinner on summer evenings and teach me the fundamentals of baseball.

"When a batter comes to the plate," he would say, "get into the ready position. Stay crouched and keep your feet spread, so you can move in any direction."

He was a baseball purist and a stickler for detail, which is probably where I get it. He taught me that if you're serious about doing anything, you've got to master the fundamentals.

When I became an adult, I often heard cops, judges, even offenders comment on what a good man he was. I will consider my life a success if people say the same of me.

Both my father and mother, the former Eleanor O'Brien, were born and raised in Jersey City and never left. I am the oldest of four children, three years older than my sister, Sheila. Then comes my brother, Brian, who is five years younger than me, and my brother Tim, nine years younger than me.

Sports was always a very important part of our lives when we were growing up. Seasonal sports. We'd play baseball in the summer, football in the fall, basketball in the winter. Both my brothers played varsity baseball and basketball in high school.

My parents worked hard to be able to afford to send each of us to Catholic schools. I went to high school in Jersey City, at St. Peter's Prep, and to college in Jersey City, at St. Peter's College. I played varsity basketball both in high school and college.

When I graduated from St. Peters, I decided to go into teaching. While I was waiting for my teacher's license, Dad suggested I go to the Hudson County Probation Office, where he heard there was an opening. I got a temporary job, and six months later I decided to take the Civil Service exam. A year later, in December of 1971, I got a permanent job with the Probation Office and I've been there ever since. I'm a Senior Probation Officer with a caseload of about 200, all of them individuals who were placed on probation for drug-related offenses.

When I was in high school, I used to watch the older guys in my neighborhood playing basketball in the playgrounds. One of them was George Blaney, who was something of a local hero as a high school star. Later, he went to Holy Cross and had an outstanding career, then played briefly for the New York Knicks before returning to Holy Cross as varsity basketball coach. He's still their coach and does a terrific job.

I bugged guys like George Blaney, Vinnie Ernst, who was an all-American at Providence, and Mike Rooney, who played at Oklahoma and St. Bonaventure and is the best pure shooter ever to come out of Jersey City, to teach me the fundamentals of the game. Each of them was very generous with his time. I learned a great deal of basketball from them.

When I was a freshman in college, my brother Brian was in the eighth grade at St. Paul in the Greenville section of Jersey City and he was playing basketball in a Catholic Youth Organization league. The coach was a fireman named George Newcombe. George couldn't always attend practice because firemen worked a couple of days on, a couple of days off, and sometimes were on duty around the clock. So he asked me if I could fill in for him and run the practices on the days he couldn't make them.

13

I started going on days George couldn't get there. Then I started going to practice on days when George was there. I made all the games. In class, instead of concentrating on my studies and lectures, I was diagramming out-of-bounds plays. I was hooked.

In 1968, John Ryan, a family friend, was coaching at St. Anthony and he needed a freshman coach, so he asked me if I was interested. I took the job and coached the St. Anthony freshmen for two years. Then I spent three years coaching the JV.

At that time, the coach was a man named Bill Brooks and he wasn't able to devote the time to coaching basketball and baseball that it required. So he decided to give up coaching basketball and concentrate on baseball. That opened up the varsity basketball coaching job. It was offered to me and I took it and I have been there ever since.

I'm fortunate that my work with the probation office can dovetail with my coaching job. I'm able to adjust my work schedule to my practice and game schedule, and I save up vacation time for the trips I take with St. Anthony or trips to watch my sons play. All in all, it's a very happy arrangement.

· · ·

I don't think I'm stretching the point to say that St. Anthony is unique. It's a 10-room school, a "mom-and-pop" high school run by the Felician Sisters.

This year, St. Anthony has a student enrollment of 276—174 boys and 102 girls. The composition of the student body is a microcosm of Jersey City itself: 155 students are black, 58 are white, 45 are Hispanic, 6 are American Indian, 6 are Asian, 3 are Haitian, and 3 are Portuguese. Although it is a Catholic school, 127 students, less than half, are Catholic.

The principal of St. Anthony is Sister Mary Felicia. The faculty consists of 5 Felician Sisters, 3 Marist Brothers, and 18 lay teachers. In addition, there are 2 diocesan priests on staff as part-time teachers, with one of them serving as school chaplain. The school has a teacher-student ratio of 1–12.

The amazing thing about St. Anthony is that they've been able to do so much with so little. The school building, on Eighth Street, in the Newport section of town, just outside the Holland Tunnel, is small and old and there are limited resources. The building is badly in need of repair, but there's no money for such things. We don't even have a trophy case to display the many athletic honors the school has earned through the years.

The school has no gym. The high school rents the Boys Club facilities for gym classes and we use White Eagle Hall, a small bingo hall, for most of our practices and for our freshman, jayvee, and girls basketball games.

It wasn't until three years ago that we finally got our own basketball court, a place to practice and play home games. Until then, we were a vagabond team. We'd practice wherever we could beg or borrow court time and we'd play "home" games at other high schools and colleges in the area, sometimes as far away as 20 or 30 miles from the school.

Then, three years ago, Congressman Frank Guarini got us into the Jersey City National Guard Armory. Three of my friends, Bob Sears, Harry Traina, and John Cicchetti, and I made a basketball court we could practice on. The four of us sanded and varnished an area of 10,000 square feet of the armory floor and made it suitable for basketball. Then we installed lights and a scoreboard and when we looked at our work, we realized we had made a basketball court that was more than adequate to practice on. We figured if we installed bleachers, we could play our home games there. So we installed the bleachers and a sound system and now St. Anthony has a home court where we have never been beaten. Our own "Field of Dreams."

Despite all these handicaps, our basketball program has sent players to schools all over the country, including Duke, Notre Dame, Villanova, Duquesne, Marquette, Seton Hall, LaSalle,

Xavier, Wagner, and Pittsburgh. Most important is the education afforded by St. Anthony. Last year, 92 percent of the graduating class went on to college.

Basketball is an important part of the St. Anthony tradition, and the daily life at the school. This season, we have 17 players on the varsity, 15 on the freshman team, and 23 on the JV team. That's 55 boys playing basketball, or a third of the school's entire enrollment of boys. In addition, we have varsity and jayvee girls teams.

St. Anthony's student body is reflective of the changing complexion of the inner city of Jersey City. When I first started coaching, it was mostly Polish, and the hardest thing was knowing how to spell the names of my players. Now, the student body is about 60 percent black. In recent years, the white enrollment has remained stable at about 35 percent.

My biggest job is to try to get the students to become academically motivated, to make them realize college is a viable alternative for them, and to keep the problems of the streets of Jersey City—and it has the same problems of crime, violence, and drugs that any major city has—out of their lives as much as possible.

Most of the team comes from Jersey City. We have two varsity players who are not. Carlos Cueto is from Union City, the next town, and Billy Lovett, is from East Orange. He has to take a bus every morning to the train station, then he takes the train that leaves him off about a half mile from the school and he walks to school from there. Every morning, in the rain and snow and the freezing cold.

We don't recruit and we don't give scholarships. All our students pay tuition, which is $1,850 a year. Many of them come from one-parent homes, mothers who work two or three jobs just to send their kids to school at St. Anthony.

· · ·

16

Bobby: St. Anthony has a great tradition. Some great players came out of the school. I think we built a solid reputation through the years. We have a good percentage of St. Anthony players who played on my dad's team and went on to play in college. Kids see that; they see all the guys playing on television, and I think that helps. The best players want to come to St. Anthony and once they get there, my dad spends a lot of time with them, working with them, and they get better. I think the coach has had a tremendous amount to do with the success of the program at St. Anthony.

. . .

As I've mentioned, about 52 percent of our students are non-Catholic, but their parents send them to St. Anthony for the discipline we provide. We're very big on discipline at St. Anthony, in the classroom and on the basketball court. I have a theory that while kids may rebel against discipline at first, down deep they really crave it.

I insist on discipline. I'm a stickler for detail. I demand promptness from my players, I insist on their undivided attention during practice. I don't want them fooling around when they're supposed to be working. And I believe strongly in the importance of repetition in basketball. You do things over and over and you do them right until they become second nature.

In my office, I have a list of what I call my "Ten Commandments." Each of my players gets a copy. It pretty much sums up my philosophy on basketball, and life.

1.   When a winner makes a mistake, he says, "I was wrong." When a loser makes a mistake, he says, "It wasn't my fault."

2.   A winner credits good luck for winning, even though it isn't good luck. A loser blames bad luck for losing, even though it wasn't bad luck.

3.   A winner works harder than a loser and has more time. A loser is always too busy to do what's necessary.

4.   A winner goes through a problem. A loser goes around it, and never past it.

5.   A winner shows he's sorry by making up for it. A loser says, "I'm sorry," but does the same thing the next time.

6.   A winner knows what to fight for and what to compromise on. A loser compromises on what he shouldn't and fights for what isn't worth fighting about.

7.   A winner says, "I'm good, but not as good as I ought to be." A loser says, "I'm not as bad as a lot of other people."

8.   A winner would rather be admired than liked, although he would prefer to be both. A loser would rather be liked than admired, and even is willing to pay the price of mild contempt for it.

9.   A winner respects those who are superior to him, and tries to learn something from them. A loser resents those who are superior to him, and tries to find chinks in their armor.

10.   A winner feels responsible for more than his job. A loser says, "I only work here."

A lot of our kids have seen violence in their lives, some of them in their own homes. Shootings and physical abuse. The whole gamut. So St. Anthony becomes something of a sanctuary for them.

There was one kid a couple of years ago who saw his mother shot by her boyfriend. And the next day he was in school. He didn't know where else to go. He figured the best place to go was to school. To a lot of our students, this is their family away from their family. And for many of them, St. Anthony is their family.

Sister Mary Alan, who is our Athletic Director, tells me these stories of kids working part-time jobs and bringing in their paychecks, $26 or $28, to apply to their tuition. Sister says the $1,850 annual tuition is about $1,000 less than it costs to educate each student.

One time a guidance counselor visited a student's home at Christmas and discovered the family had given up heat and electricity to meet the tuition payments. Another kid, James Wright, a basketball player, used to get up every morning at 5:30 and go to work in the neighborhood bar, cleaning rest rooms and mopping floors before coming to school, just to earn a little money to help pay his tuition. It paid off for him. James is on a scholarship at Wilkes University in Wilkes-Barre, Pa.

People say basketball is a black man's sport. I disagree. I think it's a poor man's sport.

Most of our kids and their families are struggling to make the tuition, but it's a commitment to them. Many of them, if not for basketball, would be in the public schools, but because they think being at St. Anthony offers an opportunity to get a college scholarship through basketball, the families are willing to roll the dice for $1,850 a year by working two and three jobs, hoping it will pay off. And it has for many of them.

One player, Terry Hunt, got a full athletic scholarship to the University of Maine although he saw minimal action in his junior year, mostly with the jayvee, and was not a starter in his senior year. He was just a good kid with a good work ethic and a bright student. Somebody from Maine saw him in the summer leagues, recognized his potential and gave him a scholarship. I like to think the fact that he came from St. Anthony had a lot to do with that.

I believe the quality of the education at St. Anthony for that four-year investment of $8,000 far outweighs the alternative of being in a public school because of the peer pressure that currently exists in the public school system. Often, in public schools, you might be subjected to ridicule for doing well academically because your buddies aren't convinced that school is important.

At St. Anthony they preach the importance and value of education. It's an accomplishment to make the Honor Roll. People pat you on the back and tell you that you did a great job. That gives the kids a sense of self-esteem and the motivation to do better. They also get motivation at home. A parent who is paying all that money expects to see results.

St. Anthony has been in danger of closing down several times for lack of funds, but it always has managed to survive. I like to think the success of our basketball program has had something to do with that.

. . .

Danny: St. Anthony would have closed a long time ago if it wasn't for my father. People send in donations because they know the job he does. The majority of the males who go to school there go because of basketball, and the school needs that tuition money. Without it, St. Anthony would close down. He's the reason the school is still open.

. . .

Our games usually will take in enough money at the door to pay the expenses for all the basketball teams, basketballs, uniforms, and so forth. Occasionally, we'll show a profit of a couple of thousand dollars. That money will go to pay for uniforms and equipment for the other athletic teams. When we're invited to play in a tournament—and we get many offers from all over the country—we go only if all expenses are paid—transportation, meals, and hotels.

When I first got there, St. Anthony already had a reputation as a good, small parochial school team. We just expanded it over the years. In my first year as head coach, 1972–73, we won the state championship. We set higher goals and kept knocking down obstacles and going on to bigger and better things, like 16 Parochial "B" State Championships, undefeated seasons in 1973–74 (32—0) and 1988–89 (32—0 in Bobby's senior year) and the mythical national high school championship, and a record of 28—2 last year, the 1992–93 season.

I think the main reason for our success in basketball is continuity. I've been doing this for 21 years and I'm established in the community as a person who's around and knows what he's doing. There's inherent respect. When kids come to school, they know there's a tradition at St. Anthony of players playing and winning, and then going on to play in college. So as time goes on, it's easier to sustain what St. Anthony does, despite the small number of students.

Now, I was looking forward to the new season with those mixed emotions of hope and expectation and that feeling of exploring the unknown that goes with coaching high school kids.

My first talk to the team was going to be just about the same as it's always been. First, set down the rules. I started with a reminder, and a mild reprimand, to get their attention.

"A couple of guys forgot their strength shoes," I said.

Strength shoes are a training device for increasing a player's jumping ability and his foot speed. A plate is installed at an angle beneath the sneaker's insole that keeps the player's heel from squarely touching the floor. It's a relatively new device and I believe it really helps improve jumping ability and quickness.

"It begins now," I continued. "You're going to have to get with the program.

"We have roughly three weeks to get ready for the opening game. Whoever we're going to play early in the season, those teams are going to be way ahead of us in the amount of practices they've had and the games they've played. So what we're going to have to do is take advantage of our opportunities. Every time we can take a practice and make it the equivalent of two practices, that's going to give us an edge."

I paused to look at the expression on their young faces. They seemed eager and wide-eyed. I figured I had their attention.

"The most important part is the thought process, as much as the physical. How much you pay attention. How quickly you grasp instructions. One of the biggest things that will help us save time is when we correct a mistake in practice, we want those things taken care of so we don't have to go over the same thing in a game situation. As each practice ends, if you don't understand something we've introduced, get one of the older kids to go over it with you. Or come to me and we'll try to get it straightened out.

"At the end of each day, start your own notebook, sit down and write down the things we covered that day that we want you to be responsible for."

I asked if there were any questions. There were none, but I could tell by the look on their faces that I wasn't losing them. So I moved ahead.

"In the next three weeks I want to convert from offense to defense faster than we have before. When we get to the offensive end of the floor and score, or the ball is stolen, or changes hands in any way, we want to become a defensive team much quicker and start pressing the opponent. We're going to pressure more than we have in the last couple of years. Full court pressure. Conversion is going to be important. The drills that take us from offense to defense are going to be significant. We know we can go from defense to offense quickly because we know that we want to fast break. But we want to make the same transition from offense to defense. We want to be a real good defensive team from the baseline to halfcourt, continually pressing and forcing our opponents to expend a lot of energy.

"We also want to be very conservative from halfcourt to the basket. We're not going to gamble. We're not going to take a lot of chances. We want to put ourselves in the position where our opponent is going to have to do a very good job to stop us from scoring.

"We're going to use a lot of players. In the beginning of practice, we'll probably rotate seven players and I'll be watching closely to see how many people are picking up what we're doing. The more people who are picking it up, the better we are because we would like to play nine or ten people in a game, especially in the first half of a game, so we can keep our energy level up and continue to run and press.

"This first practice will run from 10:30 to 1. We'll do a lot of drilling and skill work. The second practice this afternoon, we'll introduce a lot of moves that may be new to some of you."

I didn't want to give them too much to absorb on the first day, but the things I would cover in the first two practices are fundamentals, conditioning, and transition, changing from offense to defense and from defense to offense and doing it quickly. On offense, passing is what I stress most. That's the most important offensive skill for us—getting guys to look for one another, delivering the right pass, and not missing your teammate with a pass. It's all timing and good timing comes from constant repetition and practice.

At the same time, our defense is the most important part of our game and will take up much of our practice time. It's especially important in high school, when you have only 20 days to get ready for the season.

"We'll practice again tomorrow," I told them, "and Sunday and I'd like to think that by Sunday night, we've introduced 80 percent of what we're going to do for the season. Then it's a matter of what we retain. We don't want to come to practice on Monday and find we didn't hold things from today.

"Today is very important. The emphasis will be on conversion from offense to defense and from defense to offense.

"Saturday is just as important. We will emphasize our defense.

"Sunday we'll concentrate on fundamentals. "You have to separate one day from the next. How do you do that? Start your notebook. Even the older players are going to have to have notebooks for the new things we introduce.

"Your responsibilities? You're responsible every time you come to practice.

"One. Be enthusiastic. I'm not going to come to practice this year and see a group that's not enthusiastic. We want the mood of the team to be a group of people who are really happy to be at practice. This is not a class at school that you don't like. Everybody here supposedly wants to be here and I expect that kind of attitude to carry over every day.

"Two. Work extremely hard every day. I won't accept lackluster efforts. It's essential for the first few practices to set the tone for the work we will do in practice throughout the year. It's going to be very serious. We'll have our fun, but we want to make sure we're getting everything done first.

"The third area we're concerned with is that we correct mistakes.

"Fourth. We want to be in great shape.

"And fifth. We want to be fundamentally sound. If those five areas exist, and I'm happy with practice, we will play well in the scrimmages, and then build up to opening night. Three weeks and one day from today, the ball goes up and we'll find out exactly what we are, and that will be based on what we do between now and then.

"What I'm concerned with right now is your self-discipline as a player. The most difficult thing you'll do in the next three weeks is learn when to shoot and when to pass. The second most important thing is your shot selection. If you have an open shot and you pass on it, or if you take a shot with a guy in your face, then you didn't select the best shot at that time. If the game is tied and you're not the guy we're running a play for, if you shoot a jump shot on the first pass, that's not good shot selection. That

24

shot has to go into the basket for it even to be justified as a good shot.

"You have to pin down now who you are and what you can do. We're going to score in transition. We're going to score off our defense. We want to score off the offensive boards. We want to get to the free throw line. We want to be able to make open shots. All those areas give us a chance to be a good offensive team.

"The more well-rounded a player is, the more positions he can play. If I know only one position, I've limited my ability to play the minutes I'd be happy with.

"It's conceivable the only position Jalil wouldn't play is point guard. If he learns to play the two wing positions and the two post positions, that's four positions he can play. Billy or Carlos can play the 1, 2 or 3, all three perimeter positions. Justin can play 2, 3, 4 and 5. Jamar can play 2, 3, 4. Roshown 4 and 5.

"As we go down the line, if I know a guy can be a utility player and I can move him around, that makes him more valuable and it makes us a better team. The big part of your playing several positions is going to be your ability to understand the position, know the philosophy of the position, and what your responsibility is in that position. If we can do that, we're okay. The wing positions are basically the same. The post positions are basically the same. But when we get into special situations—out-of-bounds situations, dead ball situations, things like that, it gets more complicated. Then it's not how fast you are, or how high you can jump, or how strong you are, or how enthusiastic you are. It's how *intelligent* you are that counts.

"Now, when you hit the floor, remember. Enthusiasm. Correct your mistakes. Work hard. Be well-rounded."

I was finished. I looked into those faces, so young, so eager. Most of them I knew. Most of them had played for me. I felt we had potential, but I still couldn't help wondering what the season would bring.

Saturday, December 5

Through the years, I have often been asked if I have ever been offered a job coaching in college, or if I have any interest in coaching in college.

The answer is yes to the first question, no to the second.

People call me fairly regularly with offers to coach in college. I've had calls from search committees, calls from alumni inquiring if I have any interest. My answer to them always has been, and still is, I have absolutely no interest at all.

For one thing, I enjoy what I'm doing. For another, I wouldn't want to be tied down to a college coaching job, especially now with my sons playing college ball. As a parent, for me to get into college coaching and have to devote all my time to that job while my two boys are playing college ball would be completely opposite to the way Chris and I have lived our lives. We've always made every decision in our house based on our children—Bobby, Danny, and Melissa, who is eight years younger than Danny.

There was one time when I almost left St. Anthony for a college coaching job. I was all set to go. I'd even made a verbal commitment.

It happened in 1985, after I had been at St. Anthony for 11 seasons. I got a call from Pete Gillen, who had just taken the head coaching job at Xavier University in Cincinnati. I had known Pete since he coached high school ball in Brooklyn and we played against him in the Monsignor King Tournament in 1979–80. We both worked at the Five Star Basketball Camp and had remained friends over the years.

Pete went off to be an assistant coach at Villanova, then an assistant at Notre Dame but we managed to stay in touch. At Notre Dame, he was the guy responsible for recruiting David Rivers from St. Anthony. Pete's recruiting of Rivers and a few other top players helped Notre Dame's program improve under Digger Phelps, and it was because of Notre Dame's success, and Gillen's contribution to that success, that he was given the opportunity to move on. When the Xavier job opened up, Pete applied and got the job.

Pete called me and said he wanted to sit down and talk about my going to Xavier as his assistant. I was interested, so Chris and I flew out to Cincinnati and met with Pete over a weekend. He showed us around. He took us to Moeller High School, the well-known and very successful school in Cincinnati that has produced so many great athletes. He showed us the suburbs and the different neighborhoods. We became very serious about going there. We even looked at houses and schools for the kids.

We thought it was an excellent opportunity. The cost of living in Cincinnati was much cheaper than it is in the East, we figured this would be great for the kids and for us. A step up in our standard of living, so to speak. We left Pete telling him we had pretty much made up our minds that we were going to make the move.

On the plane ride home, Chris and I talked about the pros and cons of the move and we agreed there were many more pros than cons. We talked about how it was going to be a significant move for us, how it was going to be great for the children. And the more we talked about it, the more excited we both got.

Then we came home and told the kids about it, painting a very nice picture about the lovely neighborhood they would be living in, the excellent school they would be attending. Melissa was too young to understand, but Bobby was in the eighth grade, about to go to high school, and Danny was in the sixth grade.

As soon as we started talking about moving to Cincinnati, their faces dropped. Right away, we knew we had a problem.

"We don't want to live in Cincinnati," the boys said. "We want to play at St. Anthony. All our friends are here. We're city kids, we like living here. What's wrong with living here? Do you really want to go there that bad?"

After about an hour of listening to them, Chris and I realized this was not the appropriate move to make for the good of our children. More for Bobby than Danny because Bobby was about to go to high school and at that age, you don't want to put a kid into a situation he doesn't want to be in. It could affect what he does for the rest of his life. Bobby had his heart set on playing at St. Anthony and nothing we could say could change his mind.

So we decided that Cincinnati wasn't the right move and I called Pete the next day and explained that while I was flattered with his offer and would like working with him, we didn't think it was in the best interest of the family to make the move. Pete was very gracious. He said he understood and that was that. We're still good friends.

Do I have any regrets? I don't think you can ever look back in life and regret any decision you made. Who knows where I would be today if I had accepted Pete Gillen's offer. A head coach in college? Out of a job? You never know.

What I do know is that my children all are good kids. I'm not talking about basketball. If they never picked up a ball, they're good kids. They've done well in school. Certainly the way things turned out, just the fact that Bobby and Danny were able to get scholarships to good colleges has made our decision not to go to Cincinnati a good one.

· · ·

Danny: Dad loves coaching in high school. I don't think he could ever coach in college. He couldn't deal with the big egos that a lot of college players have. You know, "Yeah, I'm going to be a pro, I don't have to put up with this stuff."

In my opinion, he's the best high school coach in the country. High school coaches do a lot more actual coaching than college coaches. They have to develop players. They get players when they're raw and have to develop their skills. The high school coach makes his players. My father made my brother, he made me, he made all the other players who came out of St. Anthony.

· · ·

There have been other offers, or feelers, after the Xavier offer, some even to be a head coach, but I've resisted them all. For me to make any other decision, especially now, is unthinkable. This is the glory time, when I can flip on the TV and watch my boys play, or go see them play. If I was coaching in college, I wouldn't have been able to drive down to Philadelphia to watch them in last year's East Regional semifinal, and I wouldn't have been able to fly to Minnesota to watch Bobby play in the NCAA championship game. I would be too busy recruiting.

If I was involved in coaching in college, I wouldn't have been able to fly to Durham today, to watch Duke play Michigan in a rematch of last year's championship game.

It was a game I didn't want to miss. Michigan had been talking up the revenge motive, a chance to get even for losing in the NCAA final. Michigan is a very talented team. They started five freshmen in the championship game—the Fab Five, the press was calling them—and all five were back as sophomores, a little more experienced and just as talented. A lot of the experts were touting Michigan as the likely national champion. They were rated ahead of Duke and this was their chance to make a statement.

Bobby was uptight about the game. He knew it was going to be a big challenge for Duke. It might even dictate the tone of the entire season. As I said before, Bobby always has responded well to challenges.

I had scheduled an afternoon scrimmage for St. Anthony at Ridgewood High School, and Chris and I and a friend, Bob Hahner, had reservations on a 6:00 P.M. plane to Raleigh, where we would be met by Bobby's girlfriend, Ana Quinones, who would drive us to Durham for the game. My assistant, George Canda, took the St. Anthony team back to Jersey City in a van.

On the flight down, I kept thinking about the importance of the Michigan game, the history and background of these two teams. Duke and Michigan had played twice last season, a regular season game at Ann Arbor and the NCAA championship final. At Michigan, Bobby had played a very good game. In the championship game, he was just so-so. He didn't score very much because his shooting was off, but he did do everything a point guard needs to do, so from that perspective he was productive.

After the championship game, Jimmy King of Michigan and a few others made some comments about Bobby. "Yeah, he's okay, but he's nothing special."

About two weeks ago, we began hearing that nonsense again. Chris Webber and Jalen Rose were saying how they'd played tough games in Detroit all their lives and all the stuff they do in games is what they learned in the playgrounds of Detroit. This perception that the Michigan players had an edge on the Duke players because they had learned their basketball in the playgrounds was ludicrous, because nobody played in more playground games than Bobby. Being only six feet tall and excelling at the game, Bobby often ran out of challenges, so he would have to seek out games in order to get better. That took him all over the New York area, which I would match with any area in the country for the toughness and competitiveness of its playground basketball.

I was also annoyed that Michigan actually thought it had somebody who could cover Bobby and I knew there was nobody on the Michigan team who could stay with him on defense. I knew this was exactly the way the game was going to go—Bobby would be all over the court, passing, shooting, playing tough defense, penetrating. And he would frustrate the Michigan players once again.

As we listened to the assessment of the Duke team by the Michigan players I said to myself, this is absolutely crazy. All over the country, the media was asking a losing Michigan team to evaluate the team that beat them by 20 points for the NCAA championship. I couldn't wait to see Duke put an exclamation point on what had happened the year before.

I knew from talking to Bobby and to some Duke people and other parents of players that the Duke team felt that once again they were going to have to prove something against a team that had no respect for them. Duke had a veteran team made up of players who had won two consecutive national championships. They knew how to win. They had lost Christian Laettner and Brian Davis from the year before, but Cherokee Parks, who is 6—11 and strong, looked like he was going to be an adequate replacement for Laettner. Antonio Lang, a 6—8 junior, was going to take Davis's place. Both Hills were back, Grant and Thomas, veterans of two championships. Bobby was a year older and more experienced, and Chris Collins, son of the former all-pro and NBA coach Doug Collins, was a 6—3 freshman who could shoot and looked like he was going to help. And there was Coach Mike Krzyzewski, as good a game coach as there is in college basketball and a coach who is always well prepared and never loses his cool.

It was a rainy, windy day in New Jersey and our flight out of Newark Airport left 20 minutes late. I was beginning to worry we would be late for the game. It was after 8:00 P.M. when we landed in Raleigh, a 40-minute drive from Durham. Fortunately the starting time for the game was set back to 9:00 P.M. because it was being televised nationally. We arrived at the gym just as the ball was going up for the opening tap.

The place was alive with excitement. Cameron Indoor Stadium, which seats 9,000, was packed. At Cameron, the students surround the court, and they look for opportunities to distract the opposing team. If the opponent is quiet and businesslike, the students don't have a very good time with them. But if the opponent gives them some ammunition, like Michigan did, they'll have some fun with the visiting players, taunting and chanting and talking to them. Because the Michigan players were interacting with the Duke students, it made for a very noisy and emotional night.

The game was everything the experts predicted, and more. The atmosphere in that gym was like a championship game. Emotions were sky high, especially for a game played so early in the season. And the game went exactly as I thought it would.

Duke played brilliantly. And Bobby, I'm proud to say, was at the top of his game. Duke won convincingly, by the score of 79–68. Bobby had 20 points, five assists and only one turnover in 40 minutes, and twice when Michigan was making a run, he hit three-pointers. On defense, Jalen Rose never could get rid of him. Everywhere Jalen went, Bobby was right there. And anytime Duke needed him, Bobby was doing his thing, finding the open man, hitting a big basket, or stopping Michigan on defense. He easily was the most dominant player on the floor.

Grudgingly, the Michigan players were starting to show

Bobby some respect. But do you think we cared if they gave him any respect? They were now 0—3 against Duke.

At one point in the second half, the Duke students started getting on Chris Webber, Michigan's highly touted all-American. The students started to chant, "Marty has five, Webber has four . . . Marty has five, Webber has four."

I looked at the scoreboard and sure enough, Webber had only four points and Marty Clark, a Duke substitute, had five points.

After the game, in the press conference, Coach K gave high praise to Bobby.

"Bobby is like the Energizer Bunny," Coach K said.

His high school coach has known that for some time.

I always knew Bobby had special interests in playing basketball, but I would be lying if I said I always knew he had special talent. At least not at first. He always was so small for his age, not the kind of kid you would look at and think right away, "basketball player."

Of course, he was exposed to basketball at an early age. Bobby was born on June 28, 1971. At the time, I was an assistant coach at St. Anthony. Bobby was a year and a half when Danny came along and I was in my first year as head coach at the school. To help out at home and give Chris a break, I would take Bobby to practice. I'd take a bunch of diapers and some toys and a blanket and cart him off with me. Then I'd put him in a corner, surround him with a lot of chairs so he couldn't crawl away, assign a student manager to watch him, and go about my business of running the practice.

I have to admit that when practice ended, about two hours later, Bobby's diapers were soaking wet. I think that was the beginning of his resiliency as a basketball player—infrequent diaper changes.

It was also the beginning of his love affair with basketball. He was the original gym rat, engulfed in the game from the time he was a year and a half. By the time Danny was two and Bobby was three and a half, I'd take both of them to practice, and the two of them had a miniature basketball in their hands from the moment they could walk.

. . .

Danny: As long as I can remember I was around the game of basketball. As a little kid, I would try to do the same things my dad's high school players were doing, but I couldn't because I was too small. As I got bigger, Dad would let me take part in the shooting drills with the team.

I always liked all sports. I was a big baseball fan as a little kid. I loved the Kansas City Royals because of George Brett. I used to imitate his batting stance. I played Little League baseball, but by the time I went to high school, I was so involved in basketball the year round, I gave up baseball and concentrated on basketball.

. . .

Both Bobby and Danny just loved the game. They couldn't seem to get enough of it. They must have been thrown off every basketball court in the Metropolitan area—the Meadowlands Arena, Madison Square Garden, Seton Hall, St. Peter's, St. John's. At halftime, they'd pick up a basketball and begin shooting baskets. During timeouts, they'd run onto the court and shoot baskets, and they'd get thrown off the court. But they always went back.

They knew their way around every arena. One time, they went to see the Nets play the Pistons at the old Rutgers gym and they went up to Bob Lanier and asked him for his towel and he gave it to them. Another time, they went to see the Nets play the Celtics at the Meadowlands. They must have been about 9 and 11 at the time, and they knew their way around the building because they had been there so often. After the game, they managed to slip by the Meadowlands security and got into the Celtics dressing room.

They saw Larry Bird and asked him for his towel and he gave it to them. Then they went up to Robert Parrish and asked him for his sneakers. He refused, but they kept pestering him until Bird said, "Please give them the sneakers and get rid of them." Those sneakers are around our house somewhere.

When Bobby was 12, he went to his first basketball camp in the Poconos. One of my assistant coaches had won a free week at this camp, so he offered it to Bobby, who was eager to go. But he had never been away from home before.

Chris dropped him off on a Friday, then she went up to see him every day for four straight days, 110 miles each way.

· · ·

Chris: I missed him. And I knew Bobby was homesick. After all, he had never been away before. So I drove up to see that he was all right. On the fourth night, he said, "Mom, please stop driving up here every day. You're embarrassing me."

· · ·

Usually, when a kid goes away to a camp, he goes with a buddy, or with a group. Bobby was alone. He didn't know one kid in that camp. When it was time to go to sleep, he was still antsy and maybe a little homesick, so he would go out and jog around the camp until he was tired enough to go to sleep. Anyone who knows Bobby knows that for him to jog until he got tired would be 45 minutes to an hour. He ran and ran and ran. Most kids were dragging at the end of the day because of all the basketball they played, but he ran every night.

If there had been kids from New Jersey at the camp, he might have known them, but most of the kids were from New York and Pennsylvania. Because nobody knew him he couldn't say, "I'm a good player." A 4-foot, 10-inch, 12-year-old seventh grader? Nobody's buying that routine. But he turned out to be one of the best kids in camp for his age and size. At the end of camp, they made up camp shirts for all the kids and on Bobby's they printed, JOGGER JOE.

When Bobby entered St. Anthony, he stood only five feet four and weighed about 110 or 112 pounds. He was too small for the varsity, so he played on the JV team.

Midway through the season, we elevated him to the varsity, not because he was the coach's son, but because he was such a standout on the JV team and injuries had sidelined a few of our varsity players and we were short at the guard position. We needed a guard and Bobby was the best available.

Bobby's first varsity game was against my alma mater, St. Peter's Prep, in a game in St. Peter's gym. It was a difficult situation for him, being the coach's son, being so small and just a freshman. But he eased the situation by making the first three shots he took as a varsity player. Three set shots. Not jumpers. He had to crank them. He had to use all the force in his body just to get them up there.

What helped him, I think, was his understanding of the game because he had been around basketball since he was small. That understanding and knowledge he acquired helped him compensate for his lack of size.

When we looked at him, we figured if God was good to him and he just grew to be average height he would be able to overcome a lot of obstacles because of his knowledge of the game. We figured he had a chance to be six feet tall because I'm six feet and everybody in my family is tall. But as a 14-year-old freshman he was often giving away two or three years, six to 12 inches and 40 to 80 pounds to his opponents.

No doubt some people who came to our games would see this little scrawny kid playing and they would say, "Sure, he's playing because he's the coach's son."

It's not easy coaching your own son, but I honestly believe it was tougher on Bobby and Danny than it was on me. I probably drove them harder than I did the other players and I'm certain they felt the pressure to succeed more than other players.

. . .

Bobby: I've been around the game for as long as I can remember. That was a big advantage for me, seeing a lot of good players, and I think I understood the game well at an early age, so it was easy for me to step up to the varsity and play.

In the beginning, it was just as tough on him as it was on me. There was a lot of pressure on him. He thought I had a lot of ability and he tried to get the best out of me. If he thought I wasn't playing the way he believed I was capable of, he'd get on me. At first, it was hard for me to make the separation between father and coach and to realize what he was doing on the court was trying to make me become a better player. When he told me things, criticized things, I took them too personally. It bothered me. It got me down for a while. Then I learned to accept what he was saying and try to improve myself as a player. In my junior and senior years, we got along a lot better. By then, I came to understand what he was doing was all for my good.

I don't think I would have been the same player I am if I hadn't played for my dad. He's been my coach all my life. I wouldn't ever want to change that.

. . .

In his last game as a freshman, Bobby convinced a lot of people that he belonged. He scored 10 points and had 10 assists in the state final championship game, which we won. And he was second in the Most Valuable Player voting. As a 14-year-old freshman. A Munchkin.

By his sophomore year, Bobby grew to 5—7 and was named Player of the Year in Hudson County. As a junior, he had grown to his present height, a little over six feet, and was All-State. By now, it was obvious to people who might not have been fans of his, that Bobby deserved what he had accomplished.

I think there's always a measure of jealousy and skepticism if a kid plays for his father. I'm sure there were people who would have liked to see him fail. But in his four years at St. Anthony, our record was 115—5, a winning percentage of .960. Twice he was first team All-State, once Gatorade Player of the Year for New Jersey, and four times he helped St. Anthony win a state championship. You don't accomplish all of that because you're the coach's son. Ultimately, those people who might have been Bobby's detractors had to concede he was a pretty good player.

The junior year is an important one for a high school athlete. That's when the recruiting process really begins, and it was beginning in our house. The road that led Bobby to Duke is a long one with many twists and turns.

In his junior year, we started to hear from colleges. Most of the Big East and Atlantic Coast Conference teams. The first question they ask when they begin to check out a prospect is the academic one. That wasn't a problem. Bobby was salutatorian at St. Anthony, second in his class. His SAT score was over 1,000, which may not be great for most students, but as an athlete, in the world of basketball, he becomes a prime prospect right off the bat. Bobby might have been behind some kids athletically, but the academic picture pulled him up into a more select group.

We heard from Georgia Tech, North Carolina, Duke, Villanova, St. John's, Syracuse, and Seton Hall. Stanford and Virginia talked to us and we even were contacted by some Ivy League schools, Princeton and Penn, but we were caught in a bind there. It takes $19,000 a year to go to Princeton. We would have to pay a large part of that $19,000 and as much as we would have loved to see Bobby go to Princeton we simply couldn't afford it. But we were satisfied that at least he was going to be able to get into a good school. That would give him the chance to play at the highest level against first-rate competition.

For some time now, I've run a summer basketball camp. A lot of college coaches came that year and we had the opportunity to sit and talk with them as the recruiting process continued. Bobby played all that summer, in playgrounds all around the area, against the best players in the area. It was clear by then that of this soon-to-be senior class, Kenny Anderson of Archbishop Molloy on Long Island was the best point guard in the country, and that Bobby was better than everybody else except Kenny. Since there was only one Kenny Anderson, there were a lot of schools scrambling around to hedge their bets in case they didn't get Anderson. And we were next on their wish list. To help with the decision-making, we made a list of schools.

Since he was a little kid, Bobby's favorite school always was North Carolina. He had gone to a Carolina basketball camp and a good friend of ours, Eddie Ford, known as "The Faa," a well-known sports columnist for the *Jersey Journal*, was a Carolina guy because of his relationship with Mike O'Koren, the former Net and a North Carolina alumnus. It almost seemed that Bobby was ordained to go to North Carolina.

When we talked to North Carolina's coach Dean Smith, he made it clear that he felt he had a very good chance of getting Kenny Anderson because one of his players, Kenny Smith, had also gone to Molloy and was a close friend of Anderson. But Coach Smith said he still wanted Bobby to go to North Carolina even if he got Anderson. He said he could play both of them, but that just didn't make any sense to us, so we had to cut the cord with Carolina and move on to other schools.

In the spring of Bobby's junior year, we had visited Villanova, Syracuse, and St. John's and made numerous visits to Seton Hall because they had recruited several St. Anthony players in the past. As time went on, it looked to us like Bobby wanted to play in the Big East. Why the Big East? Because of the caliber of basketball and because it was close to home. But there seemed to be some minor problem with every Big East school.

We had visited St. John's several times and it looked like Bobby might go there. He liked their program and he knew a lot of the kids who were playing there. And Chris loved Lou Carnesecca and his assistant, Brian Mahoney. She would have been happy to have Bobby play for them.

But there was a problem. St. John's didn't have on-campus housing and that scared Chris to death. She couldn't see this kid, who couldn't even boil water, living in an apartment off campus. Plus, when you have a commuter school, the quality of campus life sometimes isn't as good as when the kids are living there all the time. Lou Carnesecca came to our summer league many times and pushed very hard for Bobby. But as much as Chris liked Lou, she couldn't resolve in her mind the fact that at St. John's, he wasn't going to be staying on campus.

When we would sit down and talk about it, we'd think about the times Bobby would come in from playing basketball and want something to eat. Chris would suggest all the things he could do to prepare himself a snack. But in our house, a snack is picking up the telephone and ordering a pizza instead of going to the refrigerator and making yourself a sandwich. And when Chris would go to the kids' room and the clothes were piled six inches high on the floor, she'd say, "Bobby, how are you going to do this? How are you going to make the adjustment when you're living in an apartment off campus?"

So, St. John's was in trouble because of Bobby's inability to cook and do laundry and pick up after himself.

As time got closer to making a decision, we still hadn't eliminated Georgia Tech and Duke, and there still was an outside chance Bobby would end up in the Big East. Now there were indications that Kenny Anderson might go to Georgia Tech, which, of course, he did. Then on the first or second weekend in September of his senior year, Bobby made his first trip to Duke.

What swung it in Duke's favor was their recruiting strategy. It was brilliant. Most schools, when they have a prospect come to visit, expect the kid to fly there on his own. They'll meet him at the airport and show him around the campus and the town, entertain him, then take him back to the airport, put him on a plane, and send him home.

Not Duke. They sent an assistant coach up to our house, picked Bobby up, and accompanied him on the flight back down.

That made a big impression. So did the way Bobby was treated during his weekend visit. The rap on Duke was the perception that it might be too preppy for Bobby, the kids might be too rich for him, and he might not be comfortable with what campus life would be like at a school like that. Nothing was farther from the truth.

When he arrived, they had Danny Ferry, who was a senior all-American and the star of the Duke team at the time, take charge of Bobby and show him around. For two days, Ferry wore a sweatsuit and a baseball cap, which suited Bobby just fine. He met the players, went to a football game, went to Coach K's house and watched basketball films and had a very enjoyable time.

On Sunday, the entire coaching staff flew back with Bobby to New Jersey to make a presentation on what they thought Duke had to offer. It's indicative of who Bobby is that they didn't come to our house. He knew I'd be at White Eagle Hall in downtown Jersey City because we take the Bingo tables down every Sunday morning and set up the basketball court, and he could get in a weight-lifting session. Then we all went to our house and the Duke coaches made their presentation.

After a while, Bobby came down stairs and said, "Dad, I've made up my mind. I want to go to Duke."

And that was it.

. . .

Bobby: Dad really helped me a great deal with the recruiting because he knows a lot of college coaches and he knows a lot

about college programs, so he had a good understanding of the process and he helped me make some good choices. But he left it up to me to make the decision. When I decided it would be Duke, I told him that's where I wanted to go and he just said, "Fine."

Why did I pick Duke? Coach K was the main factor. He was honest with me and he seemed similar to my dad in the way he coached and the kind of man he was.

· · ·

I can honestly say that Bobby never has had a single regret about his decision to go to Duke.

And with a record of 91—17, three NCAA title games, and two national championships in Bobby's first three years there, I think it's safe to say that Duke hasn't had any regrets either.

Saturday, December 19

Sister Alan said I looked like I was having cardiac arrest. Not really. That catatonic state I was in was just my usual case of pregame jitters and start-of-the-season anxiety. Happens every year.

You might call it stage fright, but it's not like an actor's opening-night jitters. An actor can control what happens onstage. He's the master of his own fate. A coach has very little opportunity to control what happens on the basketball court. Oh, I can send in substitutions to create better matchups, or get a fresh player in the game. I can make adjustments on defense, or tell them what play to run on offense when we need a score. But for the most part, it's up to the kids. They have to get the rebound, put the ball in the hoop, and expend the necessary energy to play the kind of tenacious defense I like and expect.

• • •

Bobby: Dad always gets the best out of his players. He likes working with kids and it shows. He would do anything for the guys on his team. He takes them to camp or an AAU game. He's always there to work with them. He gives a lot of his time to develop kids into basketball players. He's also very demanding. He expects the guys to play with discipline and they show that whenever they play on his team.

· · ·

Danny: As a coach, Dad's very demanding. He's a disciplinarian, but he gives you the freedom to express yourself as long as you're playing hard and playing defense and doing whatever it takes to help the team win. Then he'll give you the freedom to shoot the ball and show what you can do.

He's just a winner. Give him a minimum of talent and put him up against a team with great players and he'll win the game. He just knows how to win. He gets the most out of his players. He got the most out of my talent and Bobby's talent, and out of Jerry Walker's talent.

All the players he has coached have gone on and lived successful lives. Not just in basketball, but in life. Because of him.

· · ·

Right now, 30 minutes before the opening tap of our first game, I don't know what to expect. We've been practicing for three weeks, had a few scrimmages, and there's not much more I can do. I have to hope the guys learned their lessons well, remember what they were taught, have corrected most of their mistakes, and will not freeze once the ball goes up.

I was confident because these kids would give it their best. They were determined. This would be our first game, but this season actually began last April. We had lost to Marist High of Bayonne in the finals of the New Jersey Parochial B championship, ending a streak of nine consecutive state championships for St. Anthony. The kids were really down after that game. They knew they had not played up to their potential. They felt they had let the school, and me, down and those who were back this year vowed not to let that happen again.

Instead of brooding and feeling sorry for themselves, they made a promise to work harder this season. We had a meeting in April, went over what went wrong, and the kids all went on a weight-lifting program, determined to win back what they felt belonged to them. They made a commitment then and there, in April, to win back the state championship.

I know our team has excellent potential and some experience. The heart of the team is going to be three seniors who have already signed letters of intent to Division I schools. Jalil Roberts, who's 6—5, and is our best shooter, is going to Wisconsin to play for Stu Jackson, the former coach of the Knicks. Roshown McLoed, who's 6—8 and will have to do the bulk of our rebounding, is going to play for Brian Mahoney at St. Johns'. And our point guard, Halim Abdullah, who's 5—7, is going to play for coach Karl Fogel at Northeastern.

I figure to use eight players this season for the bulk of the time, and try to give my other underclassmen some playing time and game experience when the situation permits it. I plan to use five players up front and they will be interchangeable parts, each one capable of playing any one of the three front court positions. I'll make an exception in the case of Roshown McLeod. Because of his size, whenever he's in the game, he'll be our center.

Roberts will start at one forward with 6—3 Jamar Curry. In reserve will be Justin Fredericks, who's a 6—3 junior and figures to be one of our key players next year, and Lonce Bethea, a 6—5 senior who is an interesting story. Lonce has played only one year of organized basketball. In his first two years at St. Anthony, he was on the bowling team. Imagine, a six-foot, five-inch bowler! The only reason we got him to play basketball is because the bowling team disbanded. I asked him to come out for basketball and he did. He can be a valuable member of our team, giving Roshown or one of the forwards a rest, or filling in when somebody gets in foul trouble. It's ironic that the eighth man on my team who is going to play quite a bit this season is there only because bowling no longer exists at St. Anthony. But that's high school basketball. You use what's available.

In the backcourt, we have three players who I expect to rotate equally. Because of the defensive pressure we like to use with our guards and the up-tempo offense we like to run, all three are going to get plenty of playing time as I rotate and rest each of them. There will be some occasions, especially against smaller, faster teams, when I'll go with a three-guard offense and they'll all be in at the same time.

The three guards are Halim Abdullah, 5-7, who I said is all set for Northeastern and is the only senior among them. The others, both juniors, are 5—11 Billy Lovett and six feet Carlos Cueto, the two players on my varsity who are not from Jersey City.

Three of this year's starters, McLeod, Roberts, and Abdullah, started as juniors, but all of them were going to be asked to perform in roles they hadn't had before. Everybody is going to be asked to play a greater role than they had last year.

We're opening up with the Fourth Annual Skyline Classic, a four-team tournament held at St. Peter's College. Bayonne High School is playing in the first game against Archbishop Molloy, which is always a high school power. Jack Curran replaced Lou Carnesecca as Molloy's basketball coach about 35 years ago and he's still there. He's won more than 600 games, more than any high school coach in New York State history. He's turned out great players such as Kenny Smith, Kenny Anderson, Kevin Joyce, and a lot of others. His teams are always talented and well coached.

Our first game is against Villa Angela-St. Joseph High School of Cleveland, which won its state championship in each of the past two years.

What concerns me most is that we're late getting started because New Jersey has a later starting date for high school basketball than most states. For instance, Villa Angela-St. Joseph has played two games. Molloy has already played seven, and won them all.

Bayonne, also playing its first game, gave Molloy a game for about three quarters, but now, midway in the second half, Molloy was showing its experience and talent and was slowly pulling away. With about 10 minutes remaining in the Molloy—Bayonne game, I left to go down to our dressing room for a few last words to the team.

"Right now," I told them, "I'm confused about who should play who. We know nothing about this other team, so the early part of the game will be like a rehearsal. I know there's the element of nervousness in playing our first game and you might expend your energy on defense. I don't want tired players on the floor, so I may make a lot of substitutions.

"Our style will be tough for them to play against, even though they've played games already and we haven't. The most important stat for us is going to be defensive rebounds. We have to stay aggressive and hold them to one shot.

"Now, let's go through our warmups in a very workmanlike and enthusiastic manner. We're at a stage where there's no pressure on us. Let's get off the launching pad. When we go upstairs, let's be sure we stay together. If things don't go well, you can look at me—I'm not wearing a sweater, I should be easy to pick out—or you can look at each other.

"Let's say our prayer."

The guys huddled for our traditional pregame prayer, then ended it with a chant of "one . . . two . . . three . . . dee-fense . . ." and then we were on our way upstairs, ready to begin another season.

Actually, I shouldn't be too concerned about how we would play. We had scrimmaged well and I thought we had some depth. I felt we were going to get off the ground and start out well . . . but you never know.

What you worry about early in the season is your team getting in foul trouble, or someone pressing too much. That can affect the way a team goes in the first games. We wanted to go right out and play an up-tempo game, but it's the first game of the season, so you worry that you could get in trouble because when you play up-tempo, there's a danger of turning the ball over. And drawing fouls.

I'm never concerned with the other team's offense. We expect to stop teams. On the other hand, we're always concerned with how we mesh offensively, what kind of rhythm and feel the players have for each other. I knew that early in the season, we could depend on Jalil to get us points until everybody has his game legs—and that takes a while for high school players. If Jalil could get us a lead, our defense could take it from there.

That's exactly what happened against Villa Angela-St. Joseph's. We played extremely well, especially for a first game. We had nice balance and learned right away that Jalil was the player we could go to. He had the hot hand, scoring 27. We won, 82—60.

The next day, we met Archbishop Molloy in the finals and handed them their first loss of the season, 65—46. That gave us the Skyline Tournament championship for the fourth straight year, every year it's been played. Roshown scored 20 and Jalil had 10. The two of them shared the Most Valuable Player award and Halim Abdullah was named to the all-tournament team. So we had won our first two games, but there still was a long way to go.

Thursday, December 31

Holiday time means tournament time. School is out, so it's a good opportunity to take the team on a trip. There are college tournaments all over the country and, in recent years, some excellent high school tournaments have sprung up. This season we're invited to tournaments in Baltimore and San Diego and we have games scheduled in Rhode Island and Massachusetts.

The holidays were very rewarding for St. Anthony alumni. Duke played in the Maui Classic and won it and Bobby was named MVP. Seton Hall beat Cornell and James Madison to win the Meadowlands Tournament and Terry Dehere was all-tournament. In Madison Square Garden, Kentucky beat St. John's to win the ECAC Holiday Festival, the oldest of these Christmas tournaments, and another St. Anthony graduate, Rodrick Rhodes, won the MVP as a freshman.

We played in the Above the Rim/Reebok Classic in San Diego, and it was a good trip for the kids. That's one of the plusses about playing high school basketball and enjoying a reputation of being a good team. The trips are relatively new. When I first started coaching, a trip might mean going to New York City or Philadelphia or other parts of New Jersey. Now we get to play all over the country.

St. Anthony doesn't get paid to play in these tournaments, but all our expenses are taken care of by the tournament—air fare, first-class hotel accommodations, meals, even side trips. It's great for our young men because they get to see places in the United States outside of Jersey City and they get to compete against teams from other parts of the country. It's all part of their education, as students and basketball players. They can measure themselves against others in basketball and they're exposed to the lifestyles and customs of people in other parts of the country.

In San Diego, Chris accompanied the kids on a trip to Tiajuana, Mexico, which was quite an experience for them. She taught them how to barter with the peddlers on the street, how to negotiate a price on a watch or a handbag for their moms. They brought home some nice gifts for their families.

At the beginning of the trip, when I would ask if anybody had the time, there was maybe one or two kids who had a watch. On the way home, we were in the airport and when I asked what time it was, about 15 kids were looking at their wrists, at the $10 and $15 watches they had bought in Tiajuana. Hopefully, these watches will last them a little while.

· · ·

Chris: We drove to Tiajuana. In the past, we would park on the U.S. side and walk across the border, but this time we were accompanied by a man named Earl Woolridge, who was our un-official host on the trip. Earl owns a wonderful restaurant, the Hometown Buffet, and he graciously fed our group and helped us in any way he could.

When he heard we were planning a trip to Tiajuana, he volunteered to accompany us, which was a good idea because Earl knows the area very well. We went in several cars and we were instructed to stay close together. I was in a car with the principal, Sr. Felicia, the Athletic Director, Sr. Alan, and Margie Genovese, an assistant AD, who was driving.

We were the last car in the group and now we're in the heart of Tiajuana and the light changes. The other cars are all going through and we get a red light. But Margie's afraid to wait because the traffic is unbelievable and she's worried that we'd lose the group and never be able to find them. So, she runs the light.

Sure enough, we're pulled over by the police and I figure, this is it, we're all going to jail, we'll never get out of this. If it wasn't for the nuns, dressed in their habits, we probably would have been dragged off to jail. But the police saw them and they let us go. Maybe they figured if they put the nuns in jail, they'd be hit with some kind of curse.

We caught up with the rest of the group, parked and walked to all the bazaars and stands that they have in Tiajuana. Earl knew most of the peddlers, so he would see to it that we weren't ripped off.

The kids loved it. It took them about 10 minutes to get into the flow, but once they saw Earl bargain with them, they were into it. When they were ready to consummate a deal with a peddler, they had Earl or me or another adult nearby and if we gave them the high sign, that meant it was a good deal.

They were buying everything in sight. Watches. Blankets. Love bracelets. They had their pictures taken on donkeys. They had a ball.

Carlos Cueto bought something to eat from a street vendor and we all thought he'd get so sick, he wouldn't be able to play. But since Carlos is of Cuban descent and is familiar with that kind of food, he obviously knew what he was eating. But none of us was brave enough to venture it.

. . .

Besides bringing home some nice gifts for themselves and their families, the kids learned another lesson on their trip to Tiajuana. They saw the poverty there, the beggars on the street, people living in hovels. Our students are poor and they have problems of their own. Sometimes they think they're the only ones with those kinds of problems. But this trip put things in a different perspective for them. They saw people who were worse off than they were.

The trip to San Diego also was good competition for them, a chance to see some of the people they're going to come up against in college. That's important because when they do go to college, they're not going to be intimidated.

Our first game was against Banning High School of Los Angeles, which figured to be extremely difficult for us because we never got to see them play. It was a day of travel, then play the next day.

Banning looked extremely athletic in pregame warmups. Their size was comparable to ours. They had a very good junior guard who Cal Irvine and a couple of other schools were looking at. In fact, some college coaches I know, who knew we were going out for this tournament, asked me to take a look at this young man and let them know what I thought.

I had a little information a friend of ours had given us about the player, but not much. At least it gave us an idea on who we should assign to guard him. The only other thing we could do was watch them in warmups.

When you're playing in this situation, you try to study your opponents to see if you can pick up some characteristics. That's not the best way of preparing because you really want to watch them in game situations, but it was the only thing we could do under the circumstances.

I was expecting a difficult game. So what happens? We came out and crushed them. Held them to 28 points and they were a very talented team. I know you're saying, "Yeah, right, they're talented and you held them to 28 points." But their coach came over to us after the game and said, "Coach, we just don't face defenses like that out here. You had our guys totally flustered."

We had to come back the next day and play Monsignor Bonner of Philadelphia, which had put on a clinic in beating Camden High School of New Jersey in the first round. Monsignor Bonner had five senior starters, an experienced bunch. They looked like a team we weren't going to be able rattle and, in fact, we never got away from them. We led anywhere from 13 to 15 points for most of the game, but their maturity kept us from running away with it.

Now we found ourselves in the semifinals against Fairfax High School of Los Angeles, which has a 6—5 point guard named Robert Foster who is going to Indiana. They had a couple of other 6—5 players who were very athlctic. Fairfax is the school that produced Chris Mills of Arizona, among others.

We fell behind by 6 in the second quarter, then Carlos Cueto made one of the biggest shots of the season. He hit a 3 that took their lead from 6 to 3 and that started us on a run of 26 straight points. From being down 6, we're up 20 at halftime and we wind up beating them, 76—47.

People can't understand how the floodgates can open and close so quickly. We were rattled in the second quarter, then Carlos hits his shot, they make a mistake, we score, and now we're on a run. They start rushing things, turning the ball over, and our defense becomes more confident and more aggressive. We went on a run of dunks and really good defensive plays in transition. They're rattled. They rush and turn the ball over and we capitalize. It can happen in practically no time.

Probably the play of the season for us, certainly the play of the game, was Carlos hitting that open 3 on a beauty of a swing pass from Halim Abdullah. Bang, we hit it. Then we go after them and they crack. In three minutes, a team that should have been right there with us broke because of the pressure we put on and one big shot. That one shot may have changed our whole season.

We played the first semifinal, which gave me a chance to scout our opponent for the championship game. Jesuit High of Sacramento was playing against Mater Dei of Los Angeles, the tournament favorite. All we read and heard about out there was how we would compare with Mater Dei. I never like to get into this sort of position. It's a no-win situation. We're listening to people saying how good Mater Dei is because they're a West Coast team and we're playing in their tournament. Everybody's asking how we would match up with them, never how they would match up with us. So we just bit our tongue on the subject and let it go.

As so often happens when there's so much talk and speculation about a matchup, Mater Dei was beaten in the semifinals, and we're matched against Jesuit instead.

We almost didn't make it to the championship game on time because we got caught in typical southern California Freeway traffic and a 15-minute ride turned into a 45-minute odyssey.

We got there at game time and didn't even have time to warm up properly. That might have been a blessing in disguise. No time to warm up, no time to get nervous, and no chance to leave our game in the pregame warmup. We more than made up for it in the game.

Jesuit is an outstanding team, 15—0 and nationally ranked at the time, with a young man named Isaac Fontayne, a 6—4 forward who plays like Joe Dumars and who is going to Washington State. We had seen him get 44, 37, and 27 points in three games.

We knew Fontayne was the player we had to control, but they also had two other outstanding players, a kid named King, about 6—7 or 6—8, who plays like Tracy Murray of the Portland Trailblazers, and another kid about 6—7. They had wonderful size and they were well coached by Hank Meyers, a transplanted New Jerseyan.

This team is scoring 80—90 points a game, so we realized we were going to have to be very efficient offensively because we know this is going to be the biggest challenge to our defense to date.

We start the game and it's obvious from the tap that we're a little tentative. We're scoring, but we're not relaxed and we're turning the ball over. We're trying too hard to make big plays.

We're down by six or eight points in the second quarter, just like against Fairfax. And once again, we go on a 15—2 run just before the half, sparked by Jalil Roberts, Roshown McLeod, and Jamar Curry. At halftime, we were up by 14.

In the second half, Jesuit was knocking on the door. They made a run at us in the fourth quarter, but in the quarter, Jalil made 15 straight points. He was on fire. Everything he threw up went in. It got to the point that Jalil was playing so well, the ball was thrown down the sideline to him right in front of our bench. He was running to get out, with his back to the ball, and he didn't see it. When we yelled, "Jalil, ball!" he turned and the ball hit him right in the chest and dropped at his feet. His man dived for the ball as Jalil picked it up, took two dribbles and hit a 3.

We knew at this point, all we had to do was be real smart, just get the ball to Jalil and get out of his way. We won, 82—69, and shot 73 percent from the floor. Jalil scored 40, a career high and one of the highest single game point totals in St. Anthony history. He was named Most Valuable Player of the tournament. Jamar Curry and Roshown McLeod both made the all-tournament team. We held Isaac Fontayne to 31, which was below his average for the tournament, but hardly one of our better defensive efforts. We now had a record of 6—0.

That made it a clean sweep for St. Anthony for the holidays. Four tournaments, four championships, three MVPs.

Sunday, January 10, 1993

We have just completed a busy two days for the Hurleys, one of those weekends where our attention was split among three different places. On Saturday, I took the St. Anthony team to Newport, R.I., to play Rogers High School in an afternoon game. By coincidence, Seton Hall was playing that night in Providence, not far away. So I made arrangements to take our entire group to watch the Seton Hall—Providence game after our game, a chance to see Danny, Terry Dehere, and Jerry Walker, the three Seton Hall starters from St. Anthony.

We traveled up to Rhode Island by bus the day of the game. We left early in the morning. The trip took four hours. We checked into our hotel, relaxed for a couple of hours, then went to our game.

Before the game, one of the officials came over and said, "Coach, let's have a good game. I'm going to let you guys play today." Anytime an official says he's going to let you play, you can walk into your huddle and tell your guys the officials are going to call the game real close. What the official is doing is compensating beforehand for how he wants the game to go.

In Rhode Island, they play with a 45-second clock in high school basketball. In New Jersey, we don't use a shot clock. My first thought was that this was going to be a problem, but it wasn't because Rogers plays an up-tempo game and so do we.

The problem we did have was with the officials. This guy who said he was going to let us play called 17 fouls against us in the first half. Four of our players picked up two fouls in the second quarter. I took them out when they got their second fouls, but I had to put them back in and two picked up a third foul.

At halftime, we were up by eight, but it was a shaky eight-point lead. We had to take guys out because of the foul problem and because the game was like running a marathon. We were burning a lot of energy and in this case, we were burning fouls, and late in the game you could start losing key players and the home team has a chance to come tugging back.

There were about 3,000 people in the gym, a sellout. We had to have a lot of poise and we had to adjust to the officials, who were calling the game a lot closer than they do in New Jersey. We built our lead into double figures in the second half, which made me feel a lot better. My feeling is if we get a lead in double figures you can't beat us because our defense is so good. We won, 68—54.

After the game, we returned to the hotel, a Howard Johnson's in Newport, where the hotel management had a buffet set up for us. Our players ate for an hour and a half straight, which is not unusual for high school boys, but it embarrassed me to the point where I thought that at the breakfast buffet the next morning, they were going to put a time limit on us. Instead, they apologized for not preparing enough food the night before.

After the evening buffet, we headed for the Seton Hall—Providence game, but we didn't go the way a clear-thinking person would. Instead of going north, then northwest, what we did was double the traveling time by going southeast, then north. We turned an easy 30-minute trip into an hour and 15-minute adventure. When we got to the arena, the game had already started. Chris and I got our tickets and we let George Canda and the other coaches handle the players' tickets.

Just as Chris and I were running to our seats, Danny hit a 3. There's eight minutes left in the first half. Somebody says to us, "Danny's playing great. He has 13 points already." As he said that, Danny committed his second foul and went to the bench where he sat for the rest of the half. So we have seen him all of about 30 seconds.

Early in the second half, Danny commits his third foul. Again, he goes to the bench. He comes back and picks up his fourth foul. Seton Hall won, 91—79, and Danny scored 18, the high game of his college career. How much of it did we see? Very little. But he had a great game . . . or so people tell us.

Terry Dehere had a brilliant game. He scored 19 in the first half. Jerry Walker also got in foul trouble and sat most of the game. So who did we see? We saw Terry Dehere play a lot. We didn't see very much of Jerry Walker and we only heard about Danny playing so well, but we really couldn't say that for a fact.

We took the clear-thinking way back to our hotel and got everybody bedded down. The next morning, we all went to 10 o'-clock mass, had breakfast, then took the 45-minute drive to New Bedford, Mass., for our game against New Bedford High.

The building was packed, more than 4,000 fans, and this was an afternoon during the NFL playoffs, which were on television. We went into our locker room, and when we came out for our pregame shoot-around, we were greeted by applause from the crowd. It was a wonderful moment and something we're not used to. Back home, fans usually boo the opponent.

In Massachusetts, they play two 16-minute halves instead of four eight-minute quarters like we do in New Jersey. New Bedford was an excellent team with a couple of very good players, but we played much better than we had the day before. Nobody got in foul trouble and we had a much better flow. We won, 67—50 and were now 9—0.

I was very pleased with our performance. I felt we had learned some lessons that would help us later in the season, about playing on the road, about adjusting to different types of officiating, and being able to play games on successive days, which we were going to have to do later when our state tournament rolled around.

The team was shaping up nicely. Early in the season, we had counted heavily on Jalil Roberts to get us a lead by putting big numbers on the board. And he did a remarkable job carrying us. He got us off the ground. Because he's such a wonderful player, once the other kids got going and began contributing to our offense, Jalil could back off and be the all-around player he is, rebounding, playing tough defense, passing. He wasn't getting the high-point totals, but he didn't have to. He no longer had to be our go-to guy. It was a tribute to his unselfishness and his concept of team play that Jalil wasn't looking to score all the time. In the long run, that was going to make us a better team.

We were rated fourth in the nation by USA *Today*, behind Simon Grantz High of Philadelphia, Martin Luther King of Chicago, and Mouth of Wilson of Oak Hill, Va. I'm not very big on ratings, although I'm not entirely against them, either. How can you say a team from Philadelphia is better than a team from Chicago, or a team from Chicago is better than a team from Virginia, or a team from Virginia is better than us, when these teams never play each other? It's just one person, or a panel's, opinion.

On the other hand, anything that brings recognition and attention to high school basketball in general, and St. Anthony in particular, I'm in favor of. It's good for our game and for our kids. But to me, the only ratings that mean anything are the ones that come at the end of the season. Even then, that's still only an opinion. In college basketball, there is one poll that is the opinion of a panel of coaches, another that is a poll of writers and broadcasters. It's impossible for anyone, a coach, a writer, or a broadcaster, to see every college team in the country.

The *USA Today* high school poll is the ranking of one individual, and I know he doesn't see every high school team in the country. Nevertheless, as I said, it does give some attention to high school basketball.

I mention the high school poll here because it's tied in with the national college ratings. Today, Duke, No. 1 in the country, played Georgia Tech, No. 10, in Atlanta. We were playing in Massachusetts at the time, so I didn't get to see the game, but we kept getting updates on the bus ride home from Massachusetts. Georgia Tech scored the first 12 points and led by as many as 15. Duke came back and lost by one, their first loss of the season after winning their first 10. It also broke their 23-game winning streak, longest in the country at the time.

Bobby didn't have a very good game. He didn't shoot well. Only six-for-17 from the field, three-for-seven from the free throw line. He also took a pretty good shot from Malcolm Mackey's elbow that almost knocked him out and he had to leave the game with about three minutes left in the half. When he returned for the second half, he was still a little woozy. That's not an excuse, just a fact.

Bobby called home at one in the morning and said he was all right, but he had a bruised sternum and his ribs were sore, and probably would be for a few days. He felt worse about losing the game.

As a coach, you never like to lose a game, but if you step back and look at it objectively, that might not have been the worse thing that could happen to Duke. For one thing, it took the monkey off their back as far as the pressure of trying to protect that winning streak. For another, it dropped them in the national rankings from first to third, which would give them some incentive. And, most important, it made them realize that maybe they were not as good as they thought they were.

As a coach, you always like to have your kids just a little hungry and a little humble; it's better to be the chaser than the chased; it's good to have something to shoot for. Losing a game often can give a team a boost.

Take Seton Hall as an example. They were picked to win the Big East and to be in the top five in the nation, but they ran into Indiana in the fourth game of the season and were beaten, 78—74. It might have taught them a lesson. After losing to Indiana, Seton Hall went on to win their next 10. And Danny was the starting point guard for the last seven, taking over for Bryan Caver, who had sprained his ankle in practice.

I'm not saying Danny was responsible for Seton Hall's winning streak, but he was getting the opportunity to play, which everybody wants, and he feels he's helping the team. You want to feel like you're a part of things and right now, that's how he feels.

I was happy for him. It hasn't been easy for Danny, first playing for his father, then playing in the shadow of his older brother, an all-American. He's had to overcome a lot of obstacles to get where he is.

If there was one thing in Danny's favor, it was being the second of two sons to play for their father. Bobby blazed the trail. It was something that was new for him and new for me. We both were learning how to deal with it at the same time and it wasn't always easy. By the time Danny came along, coaching my son was not strange for me and Danny had an idea what to expect from observing me and his older brother.

But that was Danny's only advantage. He had many more handicaps. For one, he had missed his entire sophomore year with a fractured finger and that hurt him from a development and experience standpoint. With Danny sidelined by injury, we were undefeated, won the state championship, and were voted the best high school team in the country. That was Bobby's senior year at St. Anthony.

So when Danny came back for his junior year, he not only was coming back from a season of idleness because of injury, he was coming back to replace his older brother for a team that was undefeated and No. 1 in the country. It was an impossible, no-win situation for him. He never could outdo what his brother had done. The best he could do was tie it.

. . .

Danny: When I was a junior, my brother was a freshman at Duke and he was having a great year. That was my first year playing on the varsity. There was a lot of pressure on me, Bobby Hurley's younger brother, follow in his footsteps, be a great player. That year, I didn't know how to handle it. It was tough.

No other coach would have gotten out of me what my father got out of me. He worked with me day in and day out on my shooting, my defense, my ball handling. He got me to the point where I thought I was as good as anybody in the country.

I'm not saying this because he's my father. Talk to Terry Dehere or Jerry Walker. They'll tell you the same thing. Jerry will tell you he might not be in college today if he had gone to a public school instead of St. Anthony. He might be on the streets. They all have good, strong family values, but if it wasn't for my father, I don't think they'd be in the situation they're in right now.

. . .

It was inevitable that Danny would be compared to Bobby, which was unfair to Danny. He's not Bobby, he's Danny. They're different people. Danny is about two and a half inches taller, he's darker than Bobby and he's lefthanded, Bobby is righthanded. And those were only some of the differences.

Another is the way they are perceived. Danny doesn't appear

as intense as Bobby, and looks to be more of a free spirit. That's merely his outside demeanor. Believe me, inside Danny is every bit as intense, every bit as competitive as his brother. It's just that different people have different ways of showing their competitiveness.

With Bobby gone, it gave Danny a chance to get out of his brother's shadow, to be his own person. I think he felt the need to be Bobby, to do what Bobby did, but all we wanted to get from Danny was to go out and show the same improvement you want to get from anyone else. But because he's so competitive that was a hard thing for him to accept.

When you consider the obstacles he was up against—missing his entire sophomore year and all—I think Danny did a terrific job. In his junior year, we were 28—4. We won the New Jersey Parochial B state championship and went to the finals of the Tournament of Champions, which was for the overall New Jersey championship, all schools, all categories, all groups. We lost the championship game to Elizabeth High School, a school of more than 3,000 students and with Luther Wright, the seven-foot, two-inch center, who, ironically, is Danny's teammate this season at Seton Hall.

In his senior year, when Danny and Rodrick Rhodes were our two best players, we were 31—1 and voted No. 2 in the country. We won every tournament we played in and Danny was the Most Valuable Player in every tournament. We went to the Tournament of Champions and beat Seton Hall Prep for the overall New Jersey championship. Danny was MVP.

Both Bobby and Danny were the "Gatorade Player of the Year" in New Jersey. Both were MVPs of the New Jersey State finals in their senior year. In Danny's senior year, only one player was selected from the Metro area and Danny was named the Most Outstanding Player.

So, in his senior year, Danny accomplished everything Bobby

did in his senior year, except playing on an unbeaten team and being on the No. 1 high school team in the country.

In his junior year, Danny began to get his share of offers from colleges and once again we were involved in the recruiting process.

We narrowed his list to four schools—South Carolina, Davidson, Rutgers, and Seton Hall—and Danny visited each of them. A high school kid is allowed to visit five schools and we were saving the fifth spot in case another school came along late in the process.

We heard from Duke. Mike Krzyzewski talked to us about Danny going there, but we didn't think it would be something that would be in Danny's best interest. He and Bobby are only two years apart and it would be the same thing all over again, the younger brother playing in the older brother's shadow, trying to live up to what the older brother had done. If there had been a red-shirt situation, where Danny would be able to sit out a year without any loss of eligibility, that would have split it a year and put them three years apart, and it might have worked. As it was, we didn't see the sense in Danny going to Duke and repeating that situation.

Like Bobby, Danny was pretty sophisticated about the recruiting process. He sat in on a lot of the recruiting in our home with other St. Anthony players. And, of course, he was involved in the recruiting process with Bobby.

. . .

Danny: My dad tried to stay away from it. He asked me what I was interested in doing, whether I'd like to go away or stay home. He handled the preliminary stuff; when the schools got in touch, they'd go through him. He told me he was there if I needed him, but he left it up to me. The colleges came to him and he would set up interviews and trips, but he left the final decision up to me. Once I made my decision, I started playing much better. It was a great burden off my mind.

. . .

This whole recruiting business has gotten complicated in recent years, when it used to be relatively simple. There are so many restrictions now—the number of schools a kid can visit, the number of times a college coach, or his assistant, can see a kid play, what a school can give a kid in the way of souvenirs (for example, he can get T-shirts and baseball caps, but not sneakers from a college).

The biggest change, I think, is that nowadays colleges recruit players in their junior year. They scout them, make their offers, and then they have a signing date where kids commit to a college by signing a letter of intent. All that is done before their senior year. The three seniors on this year's St. Anthony team, Jalil Roberts, Roshown McLeod, and Halim Abdullah, all were signed with colleges before they even played a game as seniors.

Some think it's not fair to the players. They feel that because boys often improve and mature so much from their junior to their senior years, they would be better served to wait until they've completed their senior year before making a commitment. It might be the difference between going to a division I college or a division II college.

But colleges are making decisions about who to recruit much earlier these days. The reason they are is because of the new NCAA rules stipulating when coaches can be out recruiting. So most of the colleges make those decisions when a player is a junior so they can get the jump on the good players and the colleges don't have to wait until the last minute to know what kind of talent they have coming in. Many college coaches nowadays refuse to even look at a senior. They figure if the player is any good, his ability will have surfaced before his senior year.

High school players like this arrangement because it takes

away the anxiety about getting into college. The better players can make their decision before their senior year. What they have to do is look at the opportunity and decide if that opportunity still will be there later. Duke may come in and say to Bobby, "We're going to sign a guard. There are two other point guards we're looking at, but if you'd be willing to make a commitment right now, we'd love have you."

Bobby might know two other point guards are going to visit Duke and that opportunity might not be there for him later. So you consider the options. I think they're being honest with us, I think there's a real opportunity there, I don't want to wait. The positive part is once a kid does make a decision, as long as it's a good school and there's the opportunity to play, then it's a no-brainer.

As a parent, and a coach, I like it this way. If a player waits until his senior year, he can't enjoy that year because every time he plays, he's unconsciously aware of the fact that he's in limbo and that there are coaches in the stands that day. So he may be pressing to make a good impression. As a coach, I want him to act normal and enjoy his senior year and not feel he has to play to impress some college coach. The decision is made; now he can relax and have fun.

Take Halim, our starting point guard and a terrific player. He's already signed to go to Northeastern, so you might say if he waited he could have a terrific senior year and he might get recruited by Michigan or Kentucky or Indiana or Duke.

Well, maybe Halim is better off at Northeastern than he would be at one of those other basketball powers. He chose Northeastern because he wants engineering. If you look at each kid, there are certain academic courses that each school offers. Northeastern has a co-op education program, so Halim will go to school for five years. He'll study engineering, they'll help him get a job in the field, and he'll play basketball.

He's 5—7, so he doesn't see pro basketball in his future. But he sees engineering and the opportunity in a co-op to work each year while he's going to college and playing. He has a leg up on his future. He loves Boston. He thought it was great when he went for a visit. He thinks Northeastern's program is very solid and he felt comfortable with the coaching staff. They made him feel important. So he's happy with his decision, the pressure is off, and he's playing well for us this season without having to worry because college is taken care of.

It doesn't mean that just because a player is not at a major basketball power he can't make the NBA. The late Reggie Lewis went to Northeastern and he became a star in the NBA with the Boston Celtics.

Take Terry Dehere. If he had gone to Northeastern, he might have been another Reggie Lewis. He could have been a big fish in a little pond, and a lot of players would be happy being the big fish. You look at a Kentucky or an Arkansas or a Duke, there are 11 or 12 players on the varsity and each of them was probably a star in high school, but of those 11 or 12, one or two may be star players, some will be starters, but just role players, and the rest are substitutes who don't play much.

A lot of kids would rather be a star at Northeastern than a substitute at Duke. So you can go to Duke and get lost, or you can go to a small school and if you have the talent to play in the NBA, the scouts will find you wherever you are. It can happen. And that talent may never have surfaced in a big school. So you have a Reggie Lewis from Northeastern and a Charles Oakley from Virginia Union or a Scottie Pippen from Central Arkansas or a Dennis Rodman from Southeast Oklahoma State. All NBA stars from small schools.

Another reason colleges are recruiting kids in their junior years is that nowadays, there are not a lot of true sleepers in high school. Particularly in a school such as St. Anthony. Our players are going to get the benefit of the doubt because of all the good players that have come out of here. College coaches figure our players are going to continue to develop. They're basing their decision on the expectation that they're going to get better in their senior year.

As for so-called recruiting violations you hear so much about, it simply doesn't exist in my school because I'm so involved with the kids year round. Because we've done this for so many years, they know to have everything done through me. Recruiters are instructed to call me and if there are meetings, we have them in our house. We get the process started and then if the families want to get involved toward the end of the process—like in the summer before their senior year—they're more than welcome to do so.

When that happens, we let the families know about the number of schools that are interested in their sons, then we give them a guide to how we've done it in the past. We try to let them know that if they do take it upon themselves to handle the selection of a college, that if they open up their telephones at night, it's going to be a nightmare. They'll get no peace. Some families choose to experience the recruiting process themselves. Usually, after a week or two, it drives them nuts. College coaches call all the time. They feel they have to stay in touch because they know a rival school is calling. The phone is ringing off the hook, but nothing significant is ever said and everybody's baby-sitting the telephone. Invariably, the families come to us and say, "You handle it." And I have my own way of handling it.

First, you have to understand that college coaches are more likely to hound a parent than a high school coach. What they're doing is trying to figure which parent is going to be the most influential in the decision-making. That's the parent they're going to work, and the phone calls never stop. They're not going to do that with me, so if you can eliminate the family, with their approval, the process works better. The family isn't going to college, the son is.

I don't need to talk to some assistant college coach two or

three nights a week when all we're doing is chitchatting. Neither of us needs that. The process is going to consist of the head coach coming in, having told us he's seen the young man play, and telling us what he thinks that young man is. I'll listen very closely to find out if he's talking about the same person I am. If he says to me, "I really would like to have this player if he was a better shooter," and he's talking about my best shooter, then I realize the guy doesn't know what he's talking about and he's lost me.

What you want to do is get all the information you can. You want to feel comfortable with the staff, you want to ask questions about the team's depth chart, you want to find out how many other kids they're going to sign. You ask them what the students who played for them are doing now. You discuss a possible major course of study the boy is interested in and how strong that school is in that particular academic field. You find out about the summer job program, the study hall program, the percentage of minority students on campus. Then, if you like what you hear, you sit down with the young man and you tell him, "We've talked to 10 schools. You're allowed to choose five to visit. Which five will it be based on the information we've provided?"

If the young man says, "Mr. Hurley, I'd like to visit only two or three schools," then we'll take the three he likes and put a couple of others on the back burner in case he decides later that he needs more information. Then they start making their weekend visits. After the visits, we ask them to come home and write down all the things they liked about the school and put that away so they have it to refer to later. They go on their next visit and do the same thing. And they do that until they think they have enough information to make a decision.

Take Rodrick Rhodes, currently a freshman at Kentucky. Rod had some problems that can be attributed to early success. If you're really good in your freshman year in high school, what are you going to be able to shoot for? It's hard if you're Rodrick

Rhodes, and people are saying you're the best freshman high school player in the country, to try to reach a certain level of play. You're the standard and when you're the standard, it's hard to set a goal.

So, Rodrick was a little confused when the recruiting process began for him. People think a high school coach sometimes influences a kid to go to a certain school. What a high school coach does is influence a kid to have all the information necessary to make a decision.

In a lot of situations over the years, when a player has come back from a visit and said to me on a Sunday night or a Monday morning, "That's where I want to go," I always say to them, "I want you to talk to me in 24 or 48 hours. I want to see how you feel then, after the visit wears off."

In Rodrick's situation, as with many kids from St. Anthony, after he came back from a Seton Hall visit, he called me up and said, "Coach, I've made up my mind. That's where I want to go."

Then his aunt called up and she said she wasn't comfortable with the fact that he's made enough visits. At the time, he had visited only Ohio State and Seton Hall.

Well, Ohio State has 30,000 students and Rodrick probably felt like he was just one person in a city in which he wasn't comfortable. At Seton Hall, he knew half the basketball team, so naturally he was going to be more comfortable there.

We needed more information. After one day passed, he admitted that he didn't feel the same way about Seton Hall as he did before and that perhaps he was not ready to make a commitment. Kentucky had been pushing him hard, but he had decided at first not to visit there. Now he changed his mind and went there for a weekend. When he returned from Kentucky he came to school on that Monday morning and told all the teachers he had decided on Kentucky. So we went through the same procedure. Let's wait until Tuesday and see if you still feel the same way. On Tuesday, he still wanted to go to Kentucky. On

Wednesday, he was convinced. It was Kentucky. We sat down and I asked him if he thought he had to make any more visits. He said no. I suggested we wait one more day. We did and on Thursday, it was still Kentucky, and that's the decision he made.

A similar thing happened with Roshown McLeod, my center on this year's team. Every visit Roshown went to, that's where he wanted to go to school. He went to visit Wake Forest, the University of Florida, Arizona, and St. John's and every Monday, after the visit, he would show up at school wearing a baseball cap or a T-shirt he had gotten at the bookstore of the school he had just visited.

The teachers at St. Anthony grew tired of him wearing these caps and T-shirts and saying he liked the school he had just visited and that's where he wanted to go. He's such a young kid, just turned 17, and he was so easily influenced.

He ultimately chose St. John's because he's very close to his mom and his grandmother and at St. John's they'd be able to see him play. Also, the opportunity to play early in his career presents itself at St. Johns. Third was the financial package. Since St. John's has no on-campus housing, Roshown will get a monthly stipend for living off campus and he can live on that stipend during the school year and get a job in the summer, which will make college a little easier for him.

Roshown is happy. He's got his college taken care of, he expects to get to play early in his career, and he doesn't have to worry about spending money. St. John's is happy, too. They get a kid who's 6—8 and is only 17 and figures to improve and be a good player for them. This is another case where it worked out better that the recruiting process took place while Roshown was a junior.

I'm proud to say that my record shows I haven't favored any college. Roshown is the first player from St. Anthony to go to St. John's. I've had players from St. Anthony at Marquette, Notre

Dame, Villanova, Duke, Kentucky, Seton Hall and next year we'll have one each at Wisconsin, Northeastern, and St. John's.

St. Anthony is concerned about the choice of college our students make. They're very involved in that choice. They have an academic placement counselor, Mike McMott, who's vitally concerned about the quality of school a kid's going to. And just because St. Anthony is a Catholic school doesn't mean we try to steer our kids to Catholic colleges. We haven't.

The most important considerations are: Is the kid happy with his choice? Is the college's academic curriculum a good one and the right one for that particular student? Will he fit into the environment? Is he making the best possible preparation for his future?

I'm not naive. I'm a city guy. I know what's going on. The suits can't come in and impress me. I'm not going to be impressed.

When Bobby was a senior, people talked to me about coaching at the college level, and at the same time they're trying to recruit Bobby, they're trying to recruit Terry Dehere, they're trying to recruit Jerry Walker. If there's such a thing as a package deal, that's a major package. But that's insulting to me.

What if the three kids wind up at another school, do you still want me to coach?

If you make a decision to go along as part of a package, sooner or later you're going to be cut loose and then you're drifting. A kid's eligibility is four years. If you go into a situation like that, your employment is going to be affected by events you can't control. I'd much rather go to sleep at night knowing I'm doing what I want to do.

As a coach, it's important to give these kids a chance to be successful after college. They're not all going to be professional basketball players and if I send them to a place where they're just going to get paid and play and be done with it, they're not going to get their degrees, they're not going to get an education.

They'll fall short in life and I will have failed to do my job as a coach.

That goes for my own sons as well as every other kid who plays for me.

Sunday, January 17

We took our team on another trip, to Baltimore for the Charm City Classic. We played two games and won them both, including a victory over Baltimore's Dunbar High, nationally ranked and always a high school basketball power. Our record was now 11—0.

I don't want to go overboard yet. There's still a lot of games to play, but I have to say that this team has exceeded my expectations. Best of all, it's a good group. They work hard, they pay attention, they have a good work ethic, and they have given me very few problems. That hasn't always been the case with teams I've coached.

I have had my share of problems through the years, what coach hasn't? But by now I have established myself as a guy who demands discipline and won't take any nonsense from my players. They know if they play at St. Anthony, the rewards are going to be great. Because of what we've accomplished over the years, and the players the school has turned out, they know they're going to be noticed by the college scouts. They're going to get attention and recognition and their chances of getting a college scholarship are pretty good. Most of them have come to realize they'd be foolish to blow it.

They know that if they want to play for me, they're going to have to toe the line. My reputation precedes me. I'm a guy who once benched Jerry Walker for a county championship game because he missed a practice.

Jerry is a good kid. He started every game of his career and had never missed practice. Never even came late. But this one time he forced my hand.

Jerry's parents are divorced, so he didn't get too many opportunities to spend time with his father. This time his father had to go to Trenton to do something and he asked Jerry to go with him. In Trenton, their car broke down and Jerry couldn't get back for practice the day before the championship game. Now I have a problem.

It's not that Jerry has been a chronic latecomer or that he had given me a lot of trouble. As I said, he had never missed a practice before, and certainly spending time with his father was important. But so is practice. It's a commitment. I had to weigh the situation. I understood that when his father asked him to go with him, Jerry felt he ought to do that. But he should have emphasized to his father that he had to be back for practice because the county championship was the next day.

I didn't think his offense was serious enough for me to suspend him for the game, but he did do something wrong and he had to be punished. If I let this slide, I'm through. I never again could demand the discipline from my team that I have to have. I was willing to risk losing a championship because the alternative would be to lose my credibility.

I think you play him because there were extenuating circumstances, but I decided he wouldn't start the game. The decision was when to put him in. He didn't get into the game until there were four minutes gone in the second quarter, so Jerry missed twelve minutes. My team knows I'm a strict disciplinarian so I didn't think any of the players were going to question my decision or think I was being too soft on Jerry. And we wound up winning the game, which made it turn out all right. We won, Jerry was punished, and I didn't have to compromise myself.

As a coach, you can't allow yourself to operate on a double standard. That's why I even threw my own sons out of practice occasionally. Bobby will tell you it was more than occasionally.

· · ·

Bobby: I would never come late to practice. I'm not that stupid. But if I wasn't doing well, I was thrown out of practice as easily as anyone else. Early on, Dad was tougher on me. He used to throw me out to prove to everyone else that he was not going to treat me as a favorite. He did that a lot. Sometimes it helped him get the other guys on the team motivated. When I got kicked out of practice, they usually would respond.

· · ·

When he first came to school, Bobby obviously was going through something that was difficult for both of us. We were trying to figure out how you're supposed to handle your son being on the team in your relationship to the other players, and always make it obvious that there is no double standard. So Bobby suffered.

If somebody wasn't practicing well—like Jerry Walker's brother Jasper or Willie Banks—somebody wasn't having a very good day, I might be inclined to throw Bobby out of practice that day because he was a freshman and because he's my son.

After practice, I would tell the guys, "I threw Bobby out today, but you're the ones I should have thrown out."

I was doing it as a warning to them of what could happen if they didn't practice well, and to show I wasn't going to favor Bobby because he's my son.

As time went on, by the time Bobby was a junior, there wasn't much need to throw him out of practice because he was a good worker. And I think by then we had already established that there was no double standard because he had been thrown out of practice so many times.

One day I threw both Bobby and Danny out of practice. I got a double that day. I didn't like something Bobby did, I don't remember what, so I told him to get out of practice. Then I turned to Danny and said, "You get out, too, because you're his brother."

I was making a point.

My assistant coach at the time, Eddie Riche, swears I then turned to him and said, "And don't you pick up those two outside after practice."

Eddie later told me he had thought about giving the boys a ride home, but decided against it because he knew I would be following him to make sure he didn't.

· · ·

Danny: It was tougher on Bobby than it was on me. With Bobby, that was the first time around for him coaching his son and it was a learning experience for him. People might not understand unless they played for their dad. People might think the dad would favor the son because he wants his son to do well. Obviously, he wanted us to do well, but he was so much more demanding on us in practice. We'd have to do more than anybody else. He wanted us to be the best we could be.

If I made a mistake, as opposed to somebody else making a mistake, it would be magnified. I was thrown out of practice more times than I can count. Sometimes if I wasn't playing well I'd make facial expressions, or throw my hands in the air and say it wasn't my fault, and he'd just look at me and say, "Leave."

If the team wasn't playing well, just to make an example, he'd throw me out, to show the other guys; to get them stirred

A rare Hurley family photo, the five of us together, relaxing at home, me, Melissa, Danny, Chris and Bobby. (*Jeff Lowe/Sports Illustrated*)

The most agonizing game of our lives, our two sons, Bobby
and Danny, playing against each other in the 1992 NCAA
tournament. (*AP/Wide World Photos*)

Wherever he goes, Bobby is besieged by fans, autograph-
seekers and well-wishers.
(*AP/Wide World Photos*)

The Duke players were excited when they beat Michigan for their second straight NCAA title—and so was I. Coach Mike Krzyzewski, with Bobby at left, proudly holds the championship trophy. (*AP/Wide World Photos*)

Through the doors of St. Anthony have walked some of the finest young men, and best basketball players, it has been my privilege to have known and coached. St. Anthony doesn't have a gym, so we made our own — in a portion of the nearby Jersey City Armoy.   (*Jeff Lowe/Sports Illustrated*)

These are the six players who logged the most minutes and helped us win another state championship. (*Jerry Cuicci*)

Halim Abdullah (front)

Jamar Curry

Billy Lovett

Carlos Cueto

Roshown McLeod

Jalil Roberts with his
MVP trophy from the
Charm City Classic
tournament in
Baltimore.

The many faces of a coach
—concern, stress, pleading,
instructing, anxious. I normally
don't smile until the game
is over. (*Jerry Cuicci*)

Three St. Anthony grads helped Seton Hall win the Big East championship and the Big East tournament — Terry Dehere (left), Jerry Walker (below) and Danny Hurley. (*Jerry Cuicci*)

That's Danny sitting with Jerry Walker (above) and getting a hug from John Leahy (below) after the Pirates beat Syracuse for the Big East tournament title. (*Jerry Cuicci; AP/Wide World Photos*)

The day they retired Bobby's number at Duke. Coach K presents Bobby with the basketball from the game in which he recorded his 1,000th career assist. Below, Bobby holds aloft his framed jersey, No. 11, which happened to have been the number I wore in high school and college. (*Jerry Cuicci*)

Several carloads of folks from Jersey City came to Durham
to be there when Bobby's number was retired. Above, Bobby
shares the proud day with Chris, Melissa and me. Below,
Bobby sits with Sr. Mary Alan, St. Anthony Athletic Director,
and the school's principal, Sr. Mary Felicia. (*Jerry Cuicci*)

This was Black Saturday, a day I'd just as soon forget. Terry Dehere looks sadly at the scoreboard, which tells the story. Seton Hall lost to Western Kentucky, ending their hopes of getting to the Final Four. (*AP/Wide World Photos*)

The next
e, which
am in
trophy,
erry Cuicci)

ton Hall was eliminated,
y a total disaster. Here, Bobby
freshman point guard, Jason
calling Bobby's heir apparent.

This took some of the sting out of Black Saturday.
day, we won our third Tournament of Champions tit
gave us bragging rights as the No. 1 high school te
New Jersey. Here I am accepting the Championship
surrounded by the seniors from this year's team.

up. They would be thinking, "He threw Danny out, I'm next." It was just mind games. Those were the kinds of things he would do to show the team he wasn't playing favorites because I'm his son. I always knew what he was doing and why. He never told me, but he didn't have to. I always knew.

. . .

I guess I've always been tough on my own sons. I was trying to bend over backward not to show a double standard, and they got the brunt of it. I always have tried to keep them out of trouble and build up their competitiveness. It's not because I'm living my life through them. They wouldn't be the basketball players they are, or have the love of the game they have, if I were.

We've always been competitive in our family. When Bobby and Danny were little, the three of us would go to the playground and we'd play one-on-one basketball. Whichever of the two made the first foul shot would play me the first game, 15 baskets to win. The rules were I couldn't block their shots and I couldn't back them into the basket, I'd have to go over them. They were only about 10 or 12, but we'd have competitive games. We'd play all day long. I'd generally win all the games and then I'd let them play each other the last game and whoever won that game—usually it was Bobby since he was older—would have the satisfaction of winning at least one game.

Danny would be disgusted because he hadn't won a game all day. On the way home, I might be carrying the ball, Bobby would be walking 10 feet behind me muttering, and Danny would be 20 feet behind him dejected. We'd come into the house, the door would slam, they'd go downstairs and I'd get something to drink. Or if they weren't competitive, I'd come in the door mad at them because they weren't competitive enough, they weren't mad when they lost, they didn't care, or they were accepting losing. We wouldn't speak for about an hour, then we'd all sit down and have a family discussion. We had them quite often, when they were little kids and we came back from the playground, or after they'd get thrown out of practice at St. Anthony.

More often than not, after I'd thrown Bobby and Danny out of practice, we got the situation straightened out by the time we got out the door and everybody was in the car. If it wasn't, Chris straightened everything out at the dinner table.

· · ·

Chris: If practice didn't go well, Bob would blame it on Bobby or Danny. I could always tell by the look on their faces when they came home. But by the time they sat down to dinner, it would have to stop. In our house, nobody goes to bed mad at anyone else.

· · ·

Bobby swears he was 14 when he started beating me in those playground games, but he was 15 before he could beat me. I'll fight him on this. When he got to where he could beat me, it was time for me to cut him loose so he could play against better competition. I was playing Danny more regularly now and I would pound away on him to make him mentally tough. That's what those games in the playground were all about. I would shoot the last shot and say "game." Or I'd say, "This is the last point, who's got next game?" I would talk them through games so they would learn to play and be oblivious to what was going on around them.

That's why the trash talk of Chris Webber and the Michigan players didn't bother Bobby. By the time Bobby and Danny were in high school they were so thick-skinned, they didn't even hear trash talking in games.

Our competitiveness carried over to all sports. We're still competitive to this day. I can still throw a football better than either of them and I'm the best tennis player of the three.

. . .

Danny: Ha!

. . .

Melissa has missed most of this, but not because she's a girl. It's just that I'm too old to do what I used to do. Melissa is a very good athlete herself. She attends Our Lady of Mercy School, the same grammar school Bobby and Danny went to, and her basketball team won its division Catholic Youth Organization championship. Melissa plays forward. The first forward in our family.

She's a power player in basketball and softball. A rebounder in basketball and a power hitter and first baseman in softball. She's the biggest girl on her team, just the opposite of Bobby and Danny. They were both toward the bottom of the pack.

Chris has been very supportive. She attends every game and keeps score for us. She makes all the trips and is kind of like the den mother to our kids. She helps with the transportation, arranges for the game day meals. She tutors them when they need help with their schoolwork and chaperones them on trips and is always there to help them in any way she can, like bartering with peddlers on the streets of Tiajuana.

She's coached kids' teams and even has pinch hit for coaches in Jersey City when they couldn't get to a game on time. She's been around the game so long, more than 20 years, she can sit on the bench now and pull the strings. But she doesn't get involved in the strategy of the game and she doesn't second-guess me or suggest things, although she could. The strategy is left to me. The meals in our house go a lot better when Chris leaves the strategy to me.

Between the two of us, Chris and I have a pretty good network of friends in Jersey City. We hear things and we have been fortunate in being able to nip potential problems in the bud.

Once, I got word that one of my players, Willie Banks, was

being hassled by a group of thugs. I was told that every time Willie walked past a certain neighborhood, he was threatened, attacked, and hassled into a fight.

"Why is this happening?" I asked.

"Because he's carrying books and wearing a St. Anthony uniform."

I decided to take matters into my own hands.

One night, I drove Willie to the Currie Woods housing project and parked in front. Then I walked Willie into the front door, where this group of toughs was hanging out. I recognized a couple of them from their visits to the probation office. I walked right up to the group.

"I'm sure none of you has anything to do with this," I said, "but this young man is being hassled. If it happens once more, I'm getting a cop in this building full time. Hear?"

At first, they said nothing. Then I heard a voice sheepishly say, "We hear you."

And that was that. Willie Banks never was hassled again. He played on our basketball team and when he graduated from St. Anthony he was the number-one draft pick of the Minnesota Twins. He signed for a healthy bonus and today is considered one of the best young pitching prospects in the major leagues.

I make it a point every day to drive through the inner city, to the neighborhoods where the tough guys hang out, making sure none of my players is there. I know Jersey City. There are certain corners my players are not allowed to be on, and I tell them the playgrounds in their neighborhood where they should be playing. They shouldn't be on street corners.

One summer, I kept getting reports about one of my players. I had been told he was spending time on one particular street corner in Jersey City that was off limits to St. Anthony kids. This corner is a hot spot. Drug transactions, drive-by shootings, all sorts of things going on. A corner you don't want a high school kid hanging around. Even if he wasn't doing any of this stuff, it was inevitable that he would get in trouble.

When school started, I talked to this kid about it. Now it was October and I was coming home from work. It was a Wednesday, about five o'clock at night, and I pass by this hot spot and I see this kid standing on the corner. I drive home and call his mother and tell her I would have to remove him from the basketball program if he's on that corner again.

I was really offended by it because not only was he standing on the corner, he was wearing a St. Anthony jacket and that creates a bad impression. It reflects on the school, it reflects on me, and it reflects on all the other St. Anthony students.

I had talked to him about staying off that corner, but he hadn't done what I asked, so I removed him from the basketball program. His uncle had played for me and the family understood why I did what I did and were completely supportive of my action.

I began to hear that the kid was remorseful for what he had done. A month later, when it was time to start basketball, I allowed him to go out for the team. This was his senior year, but I told him he would never start a game because he had set a bad example for our underclassmen. At five o'clock in the evening on that Wednesday, he could have been in the library, he could have been working at a part-time job, he could have been lifting weights, he could have been in the gym. There were a lot of constructive activities he could have been doing instead of standing on a street corner. That's not only nonproductive, it's dangerous. We reinstated him after the family told us how remorseful he was and assured us this would never happen again.

The whole year, he was very productive for us. He was a good player and he kept his nose clean. We even started the recruiting process for him, which we had stopped because when colleges called to inquire about him, I had no choice but to tell them they would have to get back to us before we could say whether he had the potential to be a college player.

At the end of the season, on a Saturday night before the state championship game, we give the kids a curfew. Nobody was allowed out after 10:00 P.M. This kid lives about four blocks from the particular corner where I spotted him in October. Now it's the night before the championship game and he decides to go out to pick up some Chinese food and a movie. It's 8:15 and he's going to eat his food and watch his movie and then go to sleep.

So he leaves home and walks down Martin Luther King Drive, gets his Chinese food and his movie, and heads home. As he crosses the street, right in front of his house, a car pulls up and a guy jumps out of the car and puts a shotgun to his forehead and says, "Give it up."

When he went to the store, the kid didn't put on his St. Anthony jacket. Instead, he put on a brand new coat he had just gotten as a Christmas present and in the urban area, if you're wearing a new coat at night, it's like a neon light.

So this thug took the coat from the kid, then popped back into the car and drove away. They didn't take off racing because the utter gall of these kinds of acts is that they do it rather casually. So they rolled away and drove about three blocks and the kid could see that the car stopped at the same hot spot where he had been standing just a few months earlier.

This time he was completely innocent, but the lesson he learned is that he might have been involved in something serious if he had continued to hang out on that corner. You can get in trouble as a teenager if you're in the wrong place at the wrong time. Teenagers think they're immortal, but this can happen at anytime and you greatly increase the risk when you hang out at a place that is known for having problems.

The kid had a very poor game the next day and it was no wonder. I didn't find out about the incident until after the game. Eventually, he did receive a scholarship to college. He's finishing his sophomore year. He's playing basketball and I'm happy to say he's doing very well. But his life easily could have taken a different turn.

All it takes is one mistake for a youngster to ruin his life. That's why I have been so diligent about discipline and education. I'm proud to say all but one kid who played for me has gone on to college and 60 percent of them have graduated. It's not unusual for half of my basketball team to make the Honor Roll at school.

A good example is Jalil Roberts from this year's team. When Jalil was a sophomore, he was already such a talented basketball player that he got to start several games. But he was neglecting his schoolwork, so I called him in.

"You've flunked two subjects," I said. "You're ineligible to play until you get yourself turned around in the classroom. If you're not committed to your education, how committed can you be to this team? To play college ball, you've got to get the grades."

Jalil straightened himself out. He got his grades up and was reinstated to play. He's our leading scorer this year, was Most Valuable Player in a couple of tournaments, and was able to attract enough recognition to have been offered, and accepted, a basketball scholarship to the University of Wisconsin.

Except for coaching my own sons, my situation is no different from any other high school coach. You're dealing with kids between the ages of 14 and 18. They're no longer children, but they sure aren't adults. They're in that limbo period of life, which can be purgatory for them and anyone who has to deal with them.

Our experience at St. Anthony is that most of the kids who have had the most problems have them in their sophomore year. For every St. Anthony kid that people see playing basketball on television—and they are exceptional kids—there's a kid who sometime during his sophomore year in high school probably fell victim to peer pressure and started to do poorly in school. He starts to hang around with the wrong crowd. And no matter how you try to keep him with the team group, he leaves it. We don't have a 100 percent success rate in coaching.

You try to give a student the proper advice, but for the amount of hours you're around him, you can't impact totally on what he's going to do. The streets right now are very compelling because there's so much going on. When you compare the adventure of being on the streets with being in the house at night, studying, getting to sleep early so you're rested and ready to perform in basketball, sometimes it just doesn't seem to be equal.

I think all those former St. Anthony players who are on television are good role models for the younger kids. They can turn on the TV almost every night and see a Rodrick Rhodes, or a Jerry Walker, or a Terry Dehere, or a Danny or a Bobby, as they might be seeing themselves in a couple of years.

Wednesday, January 20

This is typical of high school basketball. We're scheduled to play Pope Paul VI in Haddonfield, N.J., which is in south Jersey near Cherry Hill, right outside of Philadelphia. It's about a two-hour drive.

The team went down in two vans, which left the school at 4:30 P.M. As I normally do, I drove down after work. When I arrived at the gym at about 6:30, I looked around at where my team usually assembles, in the stands, and I realized something's wrong. There were people missing.

My assistant coach, George Canda, comes over and informs me that one of the vans broke down and we have only seven players. It was almost game time, so what could I do? Fortunately, we had enough players to field a team and hope for the best.

I had four of my starters, Jalil Roberts, Jamar Curry, Halim Abdullah, and Carlos Cuerto, and Billy Lovett, who plays as much as a starter. But I didn't have three of my big men, Roshown McLeod, Justin Fredericks, and Lonce Bethea. I had to play Jalil at center.

At the end of the quarter, we were up by eight, but the seven players I had were getting a little tired. Finally, as the second quarter was starting, the shock troops arrived. We ended up winning 65—49, which is ironic. Our margin over Pope Paul was exactly the same with the entire team, eight points, as it was with seven players. That's what you call balance.

Sunday, January 24

St. Anthony, Duke and Seton Hall all played today, all after-noon games, so I had three games to worry about at the same time. We beat Lincroft Christian Brothers Academy, 46—29, and now stand 13—0. The news was not good on the other two fronts.

Seton Hall met North Carolina, the nation's fourth ranked team, at the Meadowlands Arena and although the Pirates gave them a battle, they were beaten, 70—66. That ended a 17-game winning streak for Seton Hall in the Meadowlands and dropped their record to 16—3.

Danny didn't have a good game. He didn't score. But you never can blame a loss on one player, which seemed to be what the crowd was doing. Danny was booed by his hometown fans, which stung him.

The main problem was North Carolina's run and jump de-fense, which is a very tough defense to play against. The way it works, they run at the ball handler with a second defensive player when the ball handler gets near the sideline or the halfcourt line or even after a timeout.

Seton Hall is a system team and what was happening, they'd come down to run their system and as soon as the Seton Hall players would get to their designated spots in the system, that's when Carolina would run at the ballhandler and double team the ball. Guards always have trouble with North Carolina's defense because they wind up being double teamed most of the time.

So Danny, playing point guard, was the player they were double teaming and he lost the ball a few times. Plus he didn't score. And I guess the frustration of the game, not being exactly a well-played game by Seton Hall, caused the fans to boo, which was very unfair and unjustified considering the circumstances.

After the game, when the writers asked him about the booing, Danny reacted in what we have come to know as typical fashion. He was up front and honest to a fault.

"I don't want to play anymore in this arena," he was quoted as saying. "I can't take it anymore. Yes, I'm hurt by that (the boos). I think it's unfair when a kid is in college and has enough pressure as it is. I enjoy playing road games 100 times more than playing here. There's so many negative people here and it's not a lot of fun."

Understand all this was said in the emotion of the moment— he's 19 years old, he had just played a game without scoring a point, his team had lost to a nationally ranked team in a tough, close game, so he felt partly responsible, and he had been booed at home.

A player on any level wants to be appreciated and understood, especially at home, and Danny was feeling like he wasn't getting any support from his hometown fans. I'm not saying he was right in what he did, complaining to the press, but I understood where he was coming from and what he was feeling.

I was unable to attend the game because of our own game with Christian Brothers Academy, but Chris went.

. . .

Chris: I left at halftime. I was there by myself and I didn't know what to do. It was so unfair. First you get mad, then you really don't know what to do. You can't stand up and yell at everyone.

There used to be games when, before I sat down, I would tell everybody around me who I was so they wouldn't say anything. When Danny was playing in Madison Square Garden in the preseason NIT, I got in my seat and there were a few business-men behind me and they were talking about the Seton Hall players and they mentioned Danny's name. I turned around and I said, "I'm Mrs. Hurley and if you have anything to say about Danny, say it now." But they were good guys.

The North Carolina game was another story. I was ready to cry. I didn't know what I might do, so I thought the best thing I could do was get up and leave, and I did.

It was hard because we took Danny to so many college games, at Duke and other places. And usually, the fans support the home team. But it's different in the Meadowlands. You're in a situation where people are betting on the games. They're really not true fans. It's a shame because these kids work very hard.

I normally speak to Danny and Bobby after every one of their games. If Danny gets home very late, he won't call until the next day. Bobby will call after every game no matter what time it is. If it's 4:00 A.M. and he's back from the road, he'll call.

Danny called that night. He was very down.

. . .

The next morning the phone started ringing in my office. A number of people called to complain about Danny getting booed. They felt it was out of order and undeserved. I also got calls from members of the media wanting to know my reaction to

Danny. I had a reaction, all right. It made my

think this was just one incident, isolated in the
game. There obviously was a lot of frustration in
the building that day for not being able to beat a team like Carolina. Hopes have been so high for Seton Hall this year, and losing
to North Carolina, with a chance to make a serious national
statement, caused frustration. And Danny became the focal
point of that frustration.

· · ·

Danny: It was my low point of the season, and the team's.
We put so much pressure on ourselves before the game because
this was a chance to get recognition by knocking off a top-rated
team. We started off badly and when that happens, things have
a tendency to snowball, and then you lose confidence in yourself.

I knew Mom was there and I wanted to make her proud of
me, but then as things started going against me, people started
saying stuff to me. In my own arena. I was thinking, "It's not
fair. This is not what I want to do with my life." It made me
depressed for a long time. I think a lot of what I was getting
from the fans was because of my last name. They single you out
because they expect so much.

I said some things to the press that maybe I shouldn't have. I
made a bigger thing out of it than it was. I got over 100 letters
from Seton Hall fans that were understanding and supportive.
Maybe what I should have said should have been clarified, that
it wasn't all the fans in the arena that day, just a few.

· · ·

Bobby: I try to call Danny at least once a week during the
season. After I heard about what happened in the North Caro-

lina game, I made a point to call him. I knew he'd be down and I thought I could help.

I told him I knew how tough North Carolina's defense is to play against, especially for a point guard. I could speak from experience because I've played against them twice a year during the regular season, then we usually play them in the ACC tournament.

I know it's been hard for Danny. I know the people in the New York area have been tough on him. It's tough playing there and it's been twice as tough on him because there are always people making comparisons between the two of us. I told him he'll be a stronger person for going through that. Part of him already knows that, but I thought I should tell him anyway.

. . .

People have a difficult time channeling their energy at a Seton Hall game. There was a lot of booing that day, not only at Danny. But because North Carolina traps, Danny was a guy who became the player on the spot. He didn't play a great deal in the game, a coach's decision, and he really wasn't that involved in the outcome of the game. Yet, he was selected by the people as the villain and he was booed.

When the newspapers contacted me, I was able to do some education for fans on how you're supposed to support a college player.

The problem is very simple. The Meadowlands is a pro arena. These were not students of Seton Hall doing the booing. These were not the true Seton Hall fans. These were people who purchase season ticket packages so they can get tickets for the NCAA tournament games at the Meadowlands and the entire college program there. These people are not there primarily supporting Seton Hall. If they were, they'd look at Danny and realize he's helped the team quite a bit this year. For the minutes he's played, at this point in the season, he leads the team in assists, he leads the team in steals, he has the highest percentage of assists to turnovers.

Some ticket holders just don't know how to behave. You'd like to take a film of the Duke crowd at Cameron Indoor Stadium and make these people watch it to observe how the crowd helps the Duke team, how it affects the opponents, how it affects the officials.

The problem with the Meadowlands is that it's not an on-campus arena. Students are not surrounding the court. The crowd at the Meadowlands is Northeastern in character, very pro-oriented. They yell at the Seton Hall players like they're yelling at the Devils or the Nets. Professional athletes. But these are not professional athletes. These are young kids.

This is not only about Danny Hurley. It's about Darryl Crist, who was booed terribly in one game. This is about other players who are not being treated like they're college athletes. These are young men.

All of the parents, John Leahy's parents and Darryl Christ's parents, Luther Wright's family and Jerry Walker's family, they're all in the stands. When their kids are being yelled at, they feel the same way I do. Except I have a forum for this. I'm not going to just sit there and tolerate somebody yelling at my son. I'm going to turn around and address it.

I'm not worried about Danny. He's resilient. He's doing the best he can to deal with something that is unfair. When adults dump on younger people, it's never going to be fair. Because of his personality and the emotional level he's at, Danny's a developing person right now. If that happened to me as late as my twenties I think I would have been crushed by it. Here's someone who's only 19, so it's going to affect him even greater than a more mature person.

There was a time Danny thought about transferring to another school, but it had nothing to do with him getting booed. It had nothing to do with basketball. It had to do with campus life, which he wasn't happy with as a freshman.

He was living in a dormitory with three other students. A very small dormitory room. None of the other kids were basketball players, so the hours Danny was keeping were entirely different from the hours his roommates were keeping and that made for a difficult situation. He also had no way of getting home. He had no transportation, so he was pretty much locked into a situation where he wasn't enjoying himself. He didn't have much companionship and he wasn't getting home very much.

Things changed this year. He has better housing. He lives in an off-campus apartment with two other guys who love basketball. Their hours are the hours he needs to keep. And he has a car, so he's able to get home more often to get a home-cooked meal and get his laundry done.

The reason a kid goes to college is for the life on campus. Basketball is going to be up and down, and it's only a few months out of the year. It's more important that a kid is content in the total college experience.

With the change in his housing situation, his car, and after that one incident at the North Carolina game, things have settled down for Danny. He has a chance to start next year, either at point guard or the No. 2 guard position. Both Danny and Bryan Caver are capable of playing either guard position. Bobby will be out of school next year, so that should help Danny because the comparisons will stop.

If he plays the No. 2 guard position, he might get compared with Terry Dehere, who is about to become Seton Hall's all-time leading scorer. I'm not taking anything away from Terry, who's a great player, but being compared to him won't be as tough for Danny as being compared to Bobby. I'm not saying Bobby is a better player than Terry, but he is Danny's brother.

. . .

On the same day Seton Hall lost to North Carolina and Danny was booed, Duke played Florida State at Tallahassee and got beat, 89-88. It dropped Duke's record to 13—3, all three losses coming in the Atlantic Coast Conference. That was already more losses than they had all last season.

With 20 seconds left and Duke up by two, Bobby's pass to Tony Lang was stolen by Florida State, which went ahead on a three-pointer. There was still 2.7 seconds remaining, but another inbounds pass, intended for Bobby, was stolen and Duke was beaten.

Coach Mike Krzyzewski had to be stunned, but after the game, he reacted with his typical class.

"We've been involved in some of the greatest games and certainly today was one of them," he said. "I thought both teams played extremely well. Geez, what a great game. I've been on the winning side to a lot of these, but you have to credit Florida State."

Later, Coach K took some of the blame for Duke's three losses.

"I don't want to get into details," he said, "but I think I could have done a better job. I think I have done an okay job."

There's a lesson to be learned in Coach K's words. It's easy to be gracious when you win. When you can be gracious in defeat, then you've done something.

Wednesday, January 27

Seton Hall went to Landover, Maryland, and their troubles continued. They lost to Georgetown by 11. This time it was another St. Anthony grad, Jerry Walker, who had the attention of the press.

"There are too many cliques on this team," Jerry said. "It's been a problem for a while. Certain guys sit over here, certain guys sit over there. We have to come together as a family."

. . .

Danny: Jerry was totally justified in what he said. I noticed it, too. We all did. Guys would go out to eat and certain guys would always be together and certain others would go their separate ways. It wasn't a racial thing. Guys just weren't getting along. As the season went on, they broke that up and I think Jerry saying what he did and making it public had a lot to do with correcting the situation.

Sunday, January 31

Three straight losses for Seton Hall, this time by nine points to Syracuse in the Carrier Dome, where the Hall never has won in 13 games. Danny scored 17 points and kept his team in the game. I take no consolation in that.

Sure, you're happy when your son has a good game, because it's better than losing and playing lousy, but it's not like winning. But it's a team game. When the team loses, everybody loses.

Once again, the writers gathered around Danny for post-game comments. I was proud of what he had to say.

"We don't have good chemistry," he said, "and if we don't get it back, we're going to be in trouble. We can definitely get it back together, but basketball has to become the most important thing in everyone's life."

Tuesday, February 2

Oh, the ups and downs of athletics. Back in the Meadowlands, Seton Hall broke its losing streak with a 90—71 victory over Providence. Terry Dehere, who had been in the worst shooting slump of his college career (17-for-50 from the field, 2-for-22 from three-point range, four straight games of less than 20 points after five in a row of over 20) broke out of it with 29 points.

The fans applauded politely every time Danny went into the game, which was some vindication for him. He also was a contributor to a 19—0 Seton Hall run that put the game away. By applauding Danny, it was as if the fans were saying they understand his position and they sympathized with it. Danny and Jerry Walker both had to leave the game in the second half because of the flu.

I've been getting to more Seton Hall games lately. What I've been doing is sitting upstairs in a box. It's enclosed and you can watch the game on closed circuit. This way I'm removed from what's going on downstairs. I'm trying to avoid hearing some of the things those "fans" have to say because I know if I do, I'm not just going to sit there. I'm going to have something to say myself.

Wednesday, February 3

A big test for Duke, playing against sixth-ranked North Carolina in Durham. The final score, Duke 81, Carolina 67, doesn't tell the story of the game, which was close until the final three minutes.

Chris drove down yesterday and I flew down and joined her for the game. The Cameron Crazies, which is what they call the Duke students who attend the basketball games, were up to their old tricks. North Carolina is Duke's fiercest rival for obvious reasons—they have been the two powerhouses of the Atlantic Coast Conference in recent years, and they're both from North Carolina, only eight miles apart.

One Duke student was dressed like Frankenstein and was wearing an Eric Montross (he's Carolina's big center) jersey.

They were ready to roar. And the Duke team gave them reason, but not at first.

Duke didn't take the lead for good until there was 6:16 left. Bobby made only four of 12 from the field, but every one was a three-pointer and every one was big. Whenever Carolina made a run, he hit a shot. He dominated the game. He also made eight-for-eight from the foul line, had seven assists, and outscored his man, Carolina's point guard, Derrick Phelps, 20—4. Late in the game, with Duke up by three, Bobby knocked down a three-pointer that built the lead to six and took the fight out of Carolina.

Later, the writers asked Grant Hill about the importance of that shot. Hill is a junior and a tremendous player who's going to make a great pro. He's the son of Calvin Hill, the former all-pro running back for the Dallas Cowboys and a fine, intelligent gentleman from Yale. As far as I'm concerned, Grant is a chip off his father's block.

"When the game is on the line like that and Bobby takes an open 3-pointer, you can pretty much count on it," Hill said. "He just gets his feet and body square. He has made so many of those big shots for us."

Friday, February 5

Just to make it a totally enjoyable week in the Hurley household, we beat Elizabeth High School, 70—54. St. Anthony is now 15—0.

Sunday, February 14

It's Valentine's Day and we're scheduled to go to Iona College for a game with All Hallows High School of the Bronx, coached by John Corey, always a power in the New York City Catholic High Schools league. At least today, I wouldn't have to divide my attention.

Duke played yesterday against Wake Forest, a team they had beaten earlier in their first meeting on the Demon Deacon's home court in Winston-Salem. In that game, the Wake Forest students got all over Bobby, as has happened to him on the road throughout his career. But they were particularly vicious in that game. So vicious, in fact, that Wake Forest coach Dave Odom wrote letters to Bobby and me apologizing for the behavior of the Wake Forest students. I thought that was a classy thing to do.

Bobby had been so riled up, he scored 20 points in the second half and at one point, stole the ball from each of Wake Forest's guards on back-to-back possessions and scored two layups. He also hit a 3 and another 2 for nine consecutive points in the span of a minute and 10 seconds.

I later heard from some of Bobby's teammates that when a timeout was called, he was such a man possessed, he came off the court and headed for the sideline looking as if he wanted to fight everybody on the Wake Forest bench. Coach K, who put his arms around Bobby, and steered him back to the Duke bench, spent the entire timeout saying, "Are you all right, Bob? Are you all right?"

The Duke players said they had never seen Bobby like that. It was as if he was in a twilight zone. He was so charged up, he was talking gibberish. And he dominated the game.

But it was a different story against Wake Forest at Duke. Maybe Bobby needs a hostile crowd to get charged up. Instead, after winning six straight, Duke was beaten, 98—86. They hadn't lost to Wake Forest in Cameron Indoor Stadium since 1985. But they played the entire second half without Grant Hill, who hurt his toe in a collision under the basket. You can't lose a player like Hill, one of the best in the country, and not suffer.

. . .

After losing four of their previous five, Seton Hall has come on to win two straight. They had to go to overtime yesterday to beat Villanova. Terry Dehere is back on the beam. He scored 24, six of them in overtime. Bryan Caver is back starting at point guard, so Danny's playing time has been reduced. But he's getting his minutes and that's all he wants.

We beat All Hallows to improve our record to 18—0.

Wednesday, February 17

Game called on account of . . . what?

We don't have a media guide at St. Anthony but we do have an official schedule. It's mimeographed on the school's stationery and if you look at it, it will show that on this date we were scheduled to meet McCorristin High of Trenton at the Jersey City Armory at 7:00 P.M. The game was canceled. Why? A good question.

We don't play in a league. We play as an independent, so we don't have a set schedule every year against the same teams. What we have to do is go out and schedule games with anybody we can. That's the reason we travel such great distances for games. We play teams from New York, teams from the Jersey shore, teams from as far away as Trenton and, of course, the several tournaments we play in every year. We don't worry too much about how good a team is. It's tough enough to get games as it is.

We had scheduled the game against McCorristin last fall. A couple of weeks into the season, we received a call from them saying they were canceling the game. No reason given. No excuse. They just didn't want to play.

I don't want to accuse McCorristin of anything because their coach is a good guy, but I do want to speak hypothetically about an ethical question: Is it ethical to duck a game with an opponent you believe is better than you are?

Let me emphasize that I'm not saying this is what McCorristin did. But, in my opinion, coaches—and I've known some— who back out of a game because they think the opponent is too tough are not doing right by their kids.

What are you telling them when you cancel a game? You're saying you can't beat this team, so we're not going to play them.

Let's assume that we are much better than the other team. I can think of a number of reasons why the coach should want to play us. For one thing, it would help his team improve for the rest of their games. You always improve when you step up to play against someone better than you.

For another, the other team has nothing to lose. If they lost to us, so what? They lost to a better team. But if they should happen to beat us, think of what that would do for those kids, how it would build their confidence. Even if they played us close, it would be a boost for their morale.

I can think of only one reason for not playing us if you think we're a better team, and that reason is purely selfish on the part of the coach. If he thinks he doesn't have a chance to win, then he's only concerned about protecting his record. He doesn't want another loss. If that's the reason, then he's thinking only of himself and not his team and that's not doing the players justice. For a high school coach, that's inexcusable.

I've taken my lumps, especially in my earlier days. I've gone into games against teams that I figured were better than us. But I looked at it as a learning experience, a chance for us to grow both as a team and as individuals. And there's always the chance we'd get lucky and beat this better team and that would be great for the kids.

I never have backed out of a game because the other team was better. And I never will.

Friday, February 19

Final score: St. Raymond's of the Bronx, 59; St. Anthony 58. Our first loss of the season after winning our first 19.

It's hard to go undefeated in any season. Somewhere along the way, a team is going to have a bad game, hit a dull spot, and lose. This was our bad game. Our only one, I hope.

The bottom line is we played a very good team, we played them in their building and we didn't execute late in the game when we had leads. A couple of calls late in the game didn't go our way, but if we had executed better down the stretch, we wouldn't have put ourselves in a position where a referee's whistle would affect the game's outcome.

After the game, I was very annoyed and I told the kids so in our dressing room. Not because we lost, but because we didn't execute end-of-the-game situations, moves that we had re-hearsed on a regular basis.

We lost our poise and that had affected the outcome, which made it easy for the kids to understand how important it is to properly execute end-of-the-quarter and end-of-the-game situations. Did they learn a valuable lesson? As a coach, you can only hope so.

You lose a game during the season, it's not a big thing. It's not a tournament game, it's not a championship game. It's just a game. Yes, it was a very frustrating loss, but it's not the end of the world. Or the end of the season. You can't expect a bunch of 16 and 17 year olds never to lose concentration during the season. It happens. It was just unfortunate that it came at the end of the game.

We practiced the next day and reviewed the mistakes we had made the night before. If you're running a play to end the quarter, you want to make sure you put the ball in the right guy's hands with the right amount of time on the clock. Strategies like that. Run the right play, remember the play, execute it, have it in the right guy's hands. If you do all that, you can live with the outcome. As a coach, that's really all you can ask.

What concerned me most was that the team would be down about losing. Kids think about going undefeated. A coach knows it's unrealistic, but every 16- and 17-year-old has dreams of never losing a game. It was important now for them to show they could bounce back from that kind of disappointment and not have it affect their next game. That's what I was going to be looking for.

Sunday, February 21

This is another of those days that gave me a chance to suffer three times. Seton Hall was playing Georgetown at the Meadow-lands in the afternoon. About two hours later, Duke was playing

North Carolina State at Raleigh. That night, we were playing in the Jersey City Armory against Cherry Hill East, coached by John Valore, who works at my summer camp and does a great job, and whose assistant, Larry Genzer, is an old Jersey City friend from my high school days.

Our game was important because we were coming off our first loss of the season. My job was to keep them "up" for the game. It was going to tell me a lot about my players to see if they could bounce back from losing.

Chris and I went to the Meadowlands to watch the Seton Hall game. Terry Dehere needed 11 points to break Seton Hall's all-time scoring record and I wanted to be there to see it. I was proud of Terry, especially in the first half when he passed up several shots to feed his teammates. He was making a statement that the team, not his record, came first. He knew he would get the record, and he did, with a foul shot five minutes into the second half. They stopped the game and presented him with the basketball as a memento.

Terry finished with 15 points, giving him 2,277 points, four more than Nick Werkman's Seton Hall record set 29 years ago. Terry also was just 70 points away from Chris Mullin's Big East career scoring record and had four games left in which to pass him.

Seton Hall beat Georgetown, 66—56, for its fourth straight win and 20th win of the season, the third straight year they had won 20 games.

I was feeling a lot better about things at Seton Hall. So much so, in fact, that I ventured out of the box upstairs and I was now sitting downstairs. But that didn't stop me from making my presence known, like wearing a St. Anthony jacket. My message: don't pick on any St. Anthony kid because I wasn't going to stand for it. Matter of fact, I wasn't going to stand for it if they started getting on any player, St. Anthony or not.

We were able to watch the first half of Duke—NC State at

home before we had to leave for the armory. This was a tough game for Duke, a nail-biter, and they were behind at halftime. Duke had lost two straight, they still were playing without Grant Hill and they were on the road. More than that, NC State was honoring the 10th anniversary of their NCAA championship. They had brought back all the players from that team, and the coach, Jim Valvano. Jim, who was battling cancer, gave a rousing speech to the crowd.

Talk about emotion. This is a game Duke could easily lose.

Chris brought a portable TV to our game and set it up right behind our bench and was glued to the set. We even had to hold up the start of our game about 10 minutes because our scorekeeper was busy watching television.

As much as I wanted to know what was happening at Raleigh, I couldn't stand there and watch Duke—NC State on television. I had to prepare my team for this important game.

As it turned out, I didn't have to watch the Duke game. I could tell how it was going just by listening to the reaction of Chris, who was only about 20 feet away. When she cheered, I knew it was good news. When she groaned, I knew it was bad. Fortunately, there were more cheers than groans, and there were a few "Atta boy Bobbys" thrown in.

Duke came on in the second half and won by nine. Bobby hit two big 3s in the second half and tied his school record with 15 assists. It was interesting that on the same day Bobby tied the Duke record for assists, his St. Anthony teammate, Terry Dehere, broke the all-time Seton Hall scoring record. I was really happy for Terry. Here's a young man who worked hard and deserves whatever honors, awards, and records he gets.

The remarkable thing about Terry is that he had to overcome several setbacks to get where he is. In his sophomore year at St. Anthony he was keeping bad hours, coming home late at night. He was playing jayvee basketball at the time and his mom called me and said, "Terry's coming home late at night. I've warned him about it, but he won't change. I'm worried that he's going to get in trouble."

I told her I'd take care of it. I called Terry in and said, "Terry, this just can't happen anymore."

He promised me it wouldn't, but a couple of weeks later, his mom called again and said he was out late again.

That simply would not do. As I've said before, if you're out on a street late at night in Jersey City, you don't have to be doing anything wrong to get yourself in trouble. I knew I had to put a stop to it for Terry's sake, so we removed him from the basketball program for about a month.

Then his mom called me again. This time she said he really missed basketball, was staying home at night, and was driving her crazy because he was around the house all the time. She asked if we could reinstate him.

On his mother's word that he had shaped up, we reinstated Terry toward the end of his sophomore year. We never had another problem with him.

In his junior year, Terry wasn't even a starter. He played quite a bit, but as a sixth man. At the time, the only college coach who showed any interest in him was my old mentor George Blaney at Holy Cross. Terry had the grades to get into Holy Cross and George thought he was going to be a late bloomer.

Terry didn't turn 17 until September of his senior year, so he was young for his class. He was a skinny kid, but you could see that he was going to have a lot of physical maturity as time went on.

With an eye on recruiting Terry, George watched him closely during his senior year, but Terry made no commitment. During that summer between his junior and senior year, Terry had just exploded. Now, all of a sudden, Dean Smith is looking at him, Terry Holland is looking at him, P.J. Carlesimo is looking at him. He had all the big schools interested, but Terry decided he

110

wanted to go to an urban campus and that's how he wound up at Seton Hall.

To tell you the truth, I never thought he was going to be this good. I knew he was going to be a good college player and that he probably would be a starter as time went on, but no one could have predicted he would improve to the point where he now has a realistic chance to be the all-time leading scorer in the Big East.

This is a young man who averaged 14 points a game in his senior year in high school, who made only 12 3s in his whole senior year, and I think in his first month at Seton Hall he made 12 3s. He's already the leading 3-point shooter in Big East history.

Terry clearly was a late bloomer. His situation was that he needed to develop physically. But the desire was always there. When you coach a long time in high school, you see a lot of things. It's hard to document, but I could always see that Terry had a look in his eyes: "I want to be good," it said. "I pay attention all the time. I love to play. I'll play endless hours. I'm smart, so I listen when the coaches tell me things and I'll understand what they're talking about. I'll lift weights. I'll practice hard. I'll shoot baskets on my own time. I'll do whatever I can to be better." And Terry Dehere has done all those things. That's why he's succeeded and that's why he deserves his success.

· · ·

Oh, yes, my fears that my kids would have a letdown after losing their first game proved to be unfounded. We were aggressive on defense, we were properly motivated, and we jumped out to a 21—point lead at halftime and beat Cherry Hill East, 78—42. Our record is now 20—1.

Sunday, February 28

It's a big day for the Hurleys. We're heading south again to watch Duke against UCLA. But this is not just a basketball game. They're retiring Bobby's No. 11 in pregame ceremonies.

It's a great honor for Bobby. He's only the seventh Duke player to have his number retired. The others are Dick Groat, Art Heyman, Mike Gminski, Johnny Dawkins, Danny Ferry, and Christian Laettner—a Who's Who of college basketball and pretty good company for a little kid from Jersey City.

My St. Anthony team was scheduled for a tournament in Washington Township, N.J., on the Thursday and Saturday before the Duke trip. We won our first game Thursday night, then played for the tournament championship last night and beat Woodrow Wilson High of Camden, 98—52. Right after the game, about 9:40 P.M., the Hurleys got in the car and headed for Durham. There was Chris, me, Melissa, and a friend, Bobby Hahner. We call him "Mousey."

Because I was still so wound up after a game, I started driving. I drove to Fredericksburg, Va., then Chris took over. When we got to North Carolina, Mousey took the wheel, and wouldn't you know it, within 10 miles, he got a speeding ticket.

It was about 2:30 A.M. and I was asleep in the back seat so I never knew about the ticket until later. But Chris told me Mousey never even tried to talk his way out of the ticket. He was so embarrassed, he didn't consider his options.

We pulled into Durham about 20 minutes to five in the morning, went to sleep and were awakened at 10:20 A.M. by the telephone ringing. People calling about tickets. People assuming we had done the normal thing and had arrived the previous evening. We had something to eat and got ready for the game, which wasn't scheduled to start until four that afternoon.

We didn't get to see Bobby until he appeared on the court for pregame practice. Then came the ceremony.

It was a very proud moment for us.

Coach K presented Bobby with a basketball from his 1,000th assist in the North Carolina State game. H. Keith Brodie, president of Duke, then brought out the framed jersey and presented it to Bobby, who gave the basketball and the framed jersey to Chris and me. Chris was crying. Bobby's actual jersey will be hung in the rafters of Cameron Indoor Stadium on the night of Duke's sports banquet.

As his high school coach, I was proud of what Bobby has accomplished on the basketball court. As his father, I am just as proud of the fact that he is only three courses short of his degree in sociology and that he will graduate with his class.

Bobby is serious enough as a student to understand that you want to get your degree as soon as you can. You don't want to appear as if you are someone who doesn't take school seriously.

Another thing I was proud of is how Bobby came to wear No. 11 at Duke. That wasn't his number at St. Anthony. I'm not good at numbers, so I had to check some pictures of the St. Anthony team in Bobby's senior year and he was wearing No. 14.

Shortly after he entered Duke, Bobby asked me what number

I wore in high school and college. I couldn't remember. It's not something that jumps out at you. So I rummaged around the house until I found some old pictures from my days at St. Peter's Prep and St. Peter's College and there I was, wearing No. 11. Maybe No. 14 wasn't available at Duke, but whatever the reason was, Bobby chose No. 11 and I thought it was a nice thing for him to do.

I don't have to tell you that we're proud of Bobby, just as we're proud of Danny and Melissa. We've been very fortunate to have good kids. But that's not to say they're perfect. They have their faults, and they have made mistakes. In fact, there was one incident that happened to Bobby last spring that caused us all some grief. I mention it here, not to embarrass Bobby, but to emphasize that he's human and he makes mistakes just like any kid his age does.

I was in my office one morning in May. It was about 10 o'clock when the telephone rang and it's Bobby. It's not unusual for him to call me, but this time I could tell there was something wrong.

He told me he had been arrested the night before for driving while impaired. It was almost as if someone had called to tell me a parent had died. It was like a knife in my heart.

On reflection, I was pleased that Bobby had the good sense to call and tell me directly, before I learned about it from television or radio or the newspapers. Because of who he is, it was certain to get a great deal of attention from the media. And it did.

Bobby had had a whirlwind and exciting few months. A lot had happened to him. He was finishing his junior year, a very good year with Duke winning its second consecutive national championship. He had just finished his exams, so he was in a mood for partying and relaxing with his friends.

This is what Bobby told me:

After exams were over, he had gone to a local pizza place on campus where he was to meet three other kids from his class, his roommate and two others. They were going to unwind from the pressure of exams with a pizza and some beers, nothing harmful, nothing thousands of other kids don't do.

They had a couple of pitchers of beer and some pizza. The season was over, so Bobby wasn't concerned about a few beers. The three other classmates had already been drinking before Bobby arrived. When it was time to leave, Bobby realized they had no car and he did, so he offered them a ride home.

Bobby figured he had only three beers in about an hour and he was okay to drive. Clearly, he was in better shape than the other three.

The pizza place is only about a mile from the Duke campus and while he was driving back to school, he saw the DWI checkpoint about a block away from the Duke campus. This is a regular occurrence with the Durham police. They often put checkpoints up near places frequented by Duke students.

Bobby could have taken another route to avoid the police, but he willingly pulled over, got out of the car and tested right on the spot because he thought he was okay. But he wasn't okay. He was right at the legal limit.

The whole thing could have been ignored but it wasn't and Bobby suddenly found out he was a national celebrity. And he was quick to discover what a situation like this could do to him and his family. By the following night, the whole country knew about it. It was a big story on national television for days, a big story about a young man going out and having three beers—a big story because of who Bobby is.

Do most college students do that? Yes. Are most college students in the fishbowl like Bobby is? No. Had I ever done the same thing? Yes. Were we devastated by it? Yes.

Bobby had to sort everything out for himself. He sorted them out and he learned an enormous lesson. In a small town, being a celebrity is a big deal. I couldn't help feeling that if this had happened to Bobby in Jersey City, nothing would have been made of it. Not because he's my son. I'm not suggesting he should have preferential treatment. But for a college student, who is mannerly, answers every question politely, and is not a problem, even if he's at the legal limit, I think a big city cop would have let him go. But in a small town like Durham, it's a different story. It was also interesting that the arresting officer got his name in every Southern newspaper that I read.

We learn from things in life. If it's going to take something like this, an event in which nobody was hurt, to make Bobby careful in everything he does, then it was a worthwhile lesson to learn. I'm not downplaying what he did. Drunk driving is a major problem in our country, but this, in my opinion, was not drunk driving.

One other good thing came out of the incident. Bobby volunteered to do community service and he fulfilled this commitment by visiting kids in hospitals, an experience he found both humbling and rewarding. In the long run, maybe it's just as well that it happened the way it did. If he had gotten away with it, it might have occurred again. As it is, a lesson clearly was learned and Bobby understands the significance of it.

· · ·

Bobby: It was embarrassing. The toughest thing I had to do was explain to my dad what happened. I knew it was going to hurt him. I feel I had let him and my mom and my whole family down. Also the basketball program at Duke. I could handle what people said, but putting my family and the school through it was not fair to them.

No question it hurt my image, but I think it made me more of a man and it taught me a lesson that will stay with me. What I tried to do was put it behind me and go on from there and I think I have done that.

· · ·

That incident is in the past now, not forgotten but forgiven, and now Bobby was in packed Cameron Indoor Stadium being honored by having his uniform number retired and we had reason to be proud of him again, as we have so often.

The game was on national television and, of course, it was another complete sellout. We had coffee that morning with Dick Vitale, who has been a big supporter of Bobby. He asked Chris and me if we would be a guest on television and we agreed.

The crowd was up for the game. When Bobby arrived, they went into this routine that they use to greet him. They stand up, extend their arms and bow from the waist as if he's some Middle East potentate.

When Chris and I were being interviewed on television, the crowd spotted us and the Cameron Crazies began chanting, "One more son . . . one more son . . ."

· · ·

Bobby: It was one of my proudest days since I put on a Duke uniform. It was great to be able to share it with my mom and dad. I promised myself I wouldn't get all choked up, and I didn't, until after the game.

It was especially nice when they gave me the framed uniform and the basketball from my 1,000th assist and I was able to go over and present them to Mom and Dad. I looked forward to doing that. My mom had tears in her eyes. She hugged me and said, "You're great, I'm so proud of you." My dad didn't say anything, but he didn't have to. The look in his eyes told me what he was thinking.

· · ·

It was amazing that with so much going on that day that Bobby was able to concentrate as well as he did. When the game started, he needed 20 assists to become college basketball's all-time career assist leader. I thought he was going to do it right there.

It was a close game and with 17:26 left, UCLA, which had trailed all game, took a one-point lead. But over the next six minutes, Duke went on a 14—4 run, capped off when Bobby found Thomas Hill with a pass and Thomas scored to put Duke ahead to stay, 58—49.

Bobby ended up with 15 assists, one short of his Duke record, and five short of the all-time NCAA record. He scored 19 points and Duke beat UCLA, 78—67.

After the game, coach K paid Bobby a nice compliment.

"You need to sit back and reflect on who has performed better than Bobby at his position in the ACC," he told the assembled media. "I don't know if there have been that many. Maybe none."

The game was over at a little after 6:00 P.M., but we didn't get out of Cameron until 7:30 or 7:45 because of the many postgame interviews. Then we went to a nice restaurant, Damon's, and had a Southern barbecue. There were about 20 of us, all from the New Jersey area. Some doctors from the Duke Medical Center had given Bobby a big cake. After dinner, we took the cake back to the hotel and were sitting in a rec room, eating cake and watching the highlights of the afternoon on Sportscenter.

The UCLA team was staying at the same hotel, the Sheraton. Jim Harrick, the UCLA coach, came over to say hello and offer his congratulations. Tyus Edney, the guard who had played against Bobby, came over and congratulated Bobby and said hello to everybody. Two other UCLA players, Eddie O'Bannon and Rodney Zimmerman, recognized Melissa and stopped her and began talking about the game. These UCLA guys were great. They are very competitive, but they also showed a lot of class, and that reflects on the school.

We broke up about 12:30 A.M., were on the road at six o'clock the next morning and made the trip without getting a speeding ticket. We got back about three in the afternoon, just in time for me to get to practice. It wasn't until after practice that I could get home and crash.

A hectic 48 hours, but it was well worth it. Besides, I'm not ready for the pipe and slippers and smoking jacket. Not yet, anyway.

Wednesday, March 3

Bobby missed by five breaking the all-time NCAA career assists record against UCLA, so we figured he'd do it in his next game, which is tonight, against Maryland. It's Senior Night and the final home game of the season, so it's an appropriate time to break the record.

I couldn't make the game because I was getting ready for our postseason tournament, but Chris is a glutton for punishment. Less than 48 hours after driving back from Duke, she was on her way back there again.

. . .

Bobby: I knew I needed just a few assists. Everybody was talking about the record. But this was an important game for us, so I just wanted to get it quick, as early as possible.

There were times this season when I was confused about my role, but I am focusing on being a leader and a point guard now and I feel good about this team. I'm doing my job. The people around me are comfortable in their roles, and no one's playing hesitantly. We have to play like we have nothing to lose, and I think lately we've been doing that.

. . .

Bobby got his fifth assist and broke the record with 11:02 left in the first half when he hit Erik Meek with an entry pass from the right wing and Meek scored. Duke beat Maryland, 95—79, and Bobby ended up with 19 points and 12 assists, giving him 1,046 assists for his career. Chris Corchiani of North Carolina State had set the record with 1,038.

Since Grant Hill went down, Bobby has stepped up his game. In the five games Hill has missed, Bobby is averaging 14 points and 13.8 assists with four double doubles (double figures in points and assists).

As a coach, I can tell you how important the assist record is. Assists bespeak many things about a player. They say he's unselfish and team oriented, that he places winning games ahead of personal point totals. Any player who gets a lot of assists could easily score many more points if he wanted to. There have to be many times when he could go up for the shot, or go to the hoop, but a good assist man looks to dish off instead of shooting himself, which always is for the betterment of the team.

People have been asking me recently how I think Bobby will do as a professional, I guess because that time is drawing near. As a father, it's hard to be objective. But as a coach, I feel I can have some objectivity.

Naturally, you think about where he'll go in the draft. Will he be a lottery pick—one of the top 11 players selected? Certainly, you think about that and it would be swell, but then you pull back because you're not talking about a seven-foot Shaquille O'-Neal, a guy who can turn a franchise around all by himself. You're talking about a six-foot point guard.

To be honest, it's hard for me to say how Bobby will do as a pro. I have some opinions, which I will share, but the fact is I have nothing to judge it on. I don't know pro basketball at all. Sure, I know high school and college basketball, but the pro game is altogether different.

From what I do know, I believe Bobby is suited to the pro game because he's fast and he can run all day. The 24-second clock is not going to be a problem for his energy level. The pace of the pro game is the pace he likes to play at. So those things would lead me to believe he's going to do well.

If you're looking for a point guard to get into a dunking contest or a body-building contest, maybe he doesn't fit those two categories. But if you're looking for a middle man on the break, a guy who will hit his open shot, one who can play defense on a ball-handler, then yes, he does those things.

He obviously would have trouble guarding a 6—4 or a 6—5 point guard, but that 6—4 or 6—5 point guard will have trouble guarding him, too. He'd have to turn it around and be chasing Bobby all over the place.

If his man drops off him and double teams another player, throw it back out to Bobby and he'll hit his shot. At the end of the game, don't leave him uncontested and give him the open shot because he'll make it. He always has loved being in the clutch situation, and he makes the clutch shot.

My feeling is when he plays, he concentrates on everybody else during the game, looking to pass and dish off, to the point where the defenses don't focus on him. He always thinks offense. Usually, it's on looking for the pass, knowing where everybody on his team is. He'll concentrate on passing first, shooting second. But he begins paying attention on shooting more as the game progresses. And because defenses don't concentrate on him shooting, he'll be open for shots late in the game and he's not afraid to take them.

People have referred to him as "a throwback." People have compared him to Dick McGuire, and somebody once called him "the Bob Cousy of the '90s."

That's not bad company to be placed in. McGuire and Cousy. A couple of Hall of Famers.

Friday, March 5

It's playoff time. What we've been aiming for all season. Two weeks of intense competition for the high schools in New Jersey. Lose and out, much like the NCAA tournament.

It's under the supervision of the New Jersey State Interscholastic Athletic Association, the NJSIAA, which was established in 1917. So this is its 75th anniversary. Let me explain how it works.

There are six classifications in New Jersey high school basketball, four in the public schools, two in the parochial schools, for boys and girls. Schools are categorized by enrollment. In the four public school groups, the largest schools are in Group IV, some with as many as 3,000 students, down to the smallest schools in Group I. The parochial schools have two groups, A and B. Group A is for the larger schools, Group B for the smaller schools.

Each group is further subdivided, the four public schools groups into North I, North II, Central, and South divisions, the two parochial school groups into North and South divisions. So there will be 12 state champions, one in each classification, six for boys, six for girls.

St. Anthony plays in the North Jersey Parochial B division. In my 21 years as head coach at St. Anthony we have played in our division championship game all 21 times. Since 1980, we have won the Parochial B state championship 11 times.

It doesn't end there. Four years ago, they started a Tournament of Champions, the six group champions competing in another lose-and-out tournament to determine the overall state champion of New Jersey, without regard to the school's size, its location, or its affiliation. So theoretically, St. Anthony with a student enrollment of 276, could play for the overall New Jersey championship against a school with a student enrollment of 3,000.

They've held the Tournament of Champions four times. St. Anthony has played in the final game three times and won it twice. We won it in 1989, with Bobby, Jerry Walker, and Terry Dehere as seniors. In 1990, Danny's junior year, we lost in the finals to Elizabeth High School, which had Luther Wright, Seton Hall's seven-foot, two-inch center. The irony of that is that Luther is from Jersey City, he went to the same grammar school as Terry Dehere and was in St. Anthony for his freshman year. Then his family moved and the commute was too much for him, so he transferred to Elizabeth High School. Had he stayed, he would have been the tallest player we ever had at St. Anthony, and who knows, we might have won the Tournament of Champions that year, too. We won it again in 1991, Danny's senior year.

Before a team can get to play for the state championship, it must get through a series of division and sectional playoffs. Any team with at least a .500 record by the February 3 cutoff date is eligible for the playoffs. The teams then are seeded according to their records, with the higher seeds getting the home court until the sectional finals, which are played at a neutral site.

This year, 15 teams qualified in our group, Parochial B. Since we had the best record of the 16, we were seeded No. 1 and will get a bye in the first round. Every other team will have to win four games to win the championship. We have to win only three. And because we are the No. 1 seed, we will have the home court advantage in all our games until the sectional finals.

Under this system, it is possible for a school to stack the deck for itself by playing most of its home games and the weaker part of its schedule before the February 3 cutoff, to be assured of getting into the tournament. Obviously, we didn't stack the deck. By the cutoff date, we had played just one home game, while playing a tough schedule. We've played in the Above the Rim Classic in San Diego. We've gone to play Rogers High School in Rhode Island and New Bedford in Massachusetts, both of whom won their state championship. We played Dunbar High School in Maryland, St. Raymond's in the Bronx, which won the New York City Catholic High Schools championship, and other teams rated in the top 25 nationally.

Strength of schedule is not taken into consideration by the seeding committee. You are seeded strictly on your won-lost record, regardless of who you play.

At this point, I don't know how far we can go. I think we have a very good team with a realistic chance of winning a state championship, maybe even getting to the finals of the Tournament of Champions. Rather than wait until I find out how far we go in the tournament, I feel I should give this team its due right here and now. They're not going to see this until the season is over, anyway.

I have enjoyed this year's team a great deal and I'm very proud of them, no matter how far they go. They try to keep a lot of the crazy things that happen away from me so I can concentrate on coaching, but this has been a relatively uneventful year as far as off-the-court incidents are concerned.

I have a very bright team. Five of the first seven players, including four starters, are in the Honors Program in school. We've got some boys who are pretty talented players, but there's no ego at all. I don't have anyone who perceives himself as a star. This is a group that has been very easy to coach.

There's always going to be some disciplinary problems. I've suspended kids for games for missing practice. One didn't go to detention, so he couldn't play in the next game. There are always a million little incidents that come up and you have to impose some discipline. If you don't, you have a problem, because they're at that knucklehead age where they're going to test the authority figures in their lives. And I believe at that age, they do it deliberately. They do it to see how much they can get away with, and to get attention.

They're going to test their parents by not coming home on time, or by getting a bad grade in school. They're going to decide, like three students did one day, to go out during lunchtime to Arby's, which is near St. Anthony, get their lunch and bring it back to school. That isn't so terrible if you're smart enough to take the Arby's out of the Arby's bag and put it in a plain, brown bag and walk into school with it. But when you carry the Arby's bag into school with you at lunchtime, you're being defiant. Everybody's going to see it and know you've been to Arby's and that just can't be overlooked. So those three were suspended from school for a day for leaving school to go and purchase lunch. At St. Anthony, the rule is you're there until dismissal.

It's always been my belief that kids want discipline. Especially those in St. Anthony. If they get discipline, it means somebody cares about them.

As we get started with our playoffs, let me run down the cast of characters of the St. Anthony Friars, the eight players who are going to play most of the time, who we're going to rise or fall with.

Our starting center is Roshown McLeod, the six-foot, eight-inch senior who will attend St. John's in the fall. Roshown has a lot of talent, but he's still just a baby. He just turned 17 and he didn't really start playing basketball until his junior year, so he has a lot to learn, and there's a lot of room for development. He's got to get tougher. He's a classic case of a big kid who had things his way because of his size. But he should get bigger and stronger and if he gets tougher, he could be an outstanding college player. I have to yell at Roshown a lot to remind him who he is and what his role is. We like him to go down low and crash the boards and operate in the low post. But Roshown sometimes gets lonely down there. He wants to come and play with the four other guys, pretend he's a little guy handling the ball. The old story of the comedian who wants to do Shakespeare and the serious actor who wants to be a comic. So, once in a while, when we have a big lead, we let him drift out and handle the ball to make him happy.

Jalil Roberts is one forward, a six-foot, five-inch senior, who will play for Stu Jackson at Wisconsin next year. Jalil is an excellent shooter. When he's hot, he can carry a team. He's scored in the 40s a couple of times this year and been MVP of tournaments. I told you earlier about how we leaned on Jalil at the start of the season, to get us leads early in games. Once the others got into the flow of the offense, Jalil became an all-around player, and a truly exceptional one. He can shoot the 3, and he can take it to the hoop. We also rely on him to crash the boards and do a big part of our rebounding. He's also an excellent defensive player who generally has to guard the other team's high scoring forward.

Jamar Curry is the other forward, also a senior. He's only 6—3, but he can jump through the roof. We have a play that we like to use the first time we get the ball. Jamar cuts to the basket, takes an alley-oop pass and jams it. It has a great psychological effect on our opponents. Jamar is a cousin of Jerry Walker. It's surprised me that Jamar was not recruited as a junior, but colleges are beginning to notice him now. He's really come on this season to become one of our steadiest and most reliable players.

There's been some interest in him lately from Champlain Junior College in Vermont and Fairleigh-Dickinson has inquired about him. We think other schools are going to get with him as time goes on, especially if he plays well in the tournament. A couple of the scouting services have listed him as one of the sleepers for colleges to look at among seniors who are not committed. We've got a few months yet, so, hopefully, someone will come forward. I think one of the reasons there hasn't been much interest is because Jamar is a forward and he's only 6—3. But if he spends the summer improving his shooting, which I know he will do, Jamar can be a No. 2 guard in college, and he'll make somebody a fine player.

Our senior guard and captain is Halim Abdullah. He runs the show. He's only five feet, seven inches, but he's quick and intelligent. Halim is all set to go to Northeastern next season.

Carlos Cueto is our other guard, and the only junior among the starters. He's six feet, one inch, and fast. He can penetrate and he's an excellent shooter, better than 50 percent from three-point range. He reminds me a lot of Bobby in the way he plays the game, his speed, his defense and his vision on the court, always looking for a teammate to pass to. When Carlos was a sophomore, his friends advised him to transfer to another school, where he would have a better chance to start. He thought about it, but decided to stay at St. Anthony. He spent the summer working on his game. He'd go to a gym, or to the playground, and shoot baskets until midnight, just to improve his shooting. And he did. This is the time when college coaches start looking at the juniors. They do some evaluating and they look for academic information to see if they can recruit a kid. With the new NCAA rules in effect this year, a kid can't visit a college campus until he has his SAT scores. Carlos scored 1,000 in the SAT as a sophomore and he's No. 1 in his class. The Ivy Leagues are looking at him. Harvard has expressed interest in Carlos and I'm just so happy for him. What a wonderful thing it would be if he got to go to Harvard, and all because of basketball. This is a kid who comes from a home where the primary language is Spanish. He wants to be better in every thing he does. I never see him off the court when he isn't reading a book. He's intelligent, very coachable, and never a problem. And he has a chance to be an outstanding point guard in college.

Billy Lovett is another junior guard, five feet eleven. He and Carlos are going to be my senior captains next year. Billy loves to play and he loves to be in clutch situations. He's fifth in his class, so he and Carlos are going to be recruited because they can play and they're both excellent students.

Lonce Bethea is a 6—5 senior, the former bowler who is our backup center. He hasn't had a chance to play a lot this year and it's not easy being a senior and sitting on the bench. But Lonce never complains and he does the job when he's asked to. There are a couple of Division III colleges and junior colleges recruiting him right now.

Our eighth man, who will get to play quite a bit, is Justin Frederick, a 6—4 junior who will come off the bench if any of our front-line players need a rest or get in foul trouble and we need size. With more work, athletically and academically, Justin could be a top recruit next year.

With our 22—1 record and the No. 1 seed in the North Jersey Parochial B tournament, we got a bye in the first round. Our first game tonight is against Don Bosco Tech in the Jersey City Armory.

We controlled the tip and set up for our alley-oop play. Halim threw it perfectly above the rim. Jamar Curry broke at the right time, went high in the air and jammed it in. That got our crowd into the game and effectively intimidated our opponents.

We opened a 36—9 lead in the second quarter and went on to win, 78—24. I was able to get all 18 of my players into the game. Four of our guys scored in double figures—Roshown McLeod 18, Jalil Roberts 16, Halim Abdullah 11, and Jamar

Curry 10. Halim also had six assists and five steals. Carlos Cueto had nine assists.

Now, the fun part was over. Our next game, in the North Jersey Parochial B semifinals, was going to be against Marist, which beat us last year in the division finals and ended our run of nine straight division championships. Most people think we're the two best teams in the division, but the luck of the draw had us meeting in the semis this year instead of the finals.

Saturday, March 6

Seton Hall played St. John's at the Meadowlands this afternoon for the Big East regular season championship. Before the game, they retired Terry Dehere's No. 24. So in the same week, Bobby and Terry both had their numbers retired. I was a very proud father and a very proud high school coach.

The game would determine the champion of the Big East regular season and the No. 1 seed in the Big East tournament. It was a surprise that St. John's would have been playing in the final regular season game with a chance to win the championship. The Redmen had been picked to finish ninth in the 10-team field in the preseason polls, once again showing how inconclusive polls are. But under Brian Mahoney, in his first year as head coach and replacing the legendary Lou Carnesecca, St. John's had had an excellent season.

But Seton Hall seemed to have the Redmen's number. The Pirates scored the first six points, went out to a 22—11 lead and were up by 40 26 at halftime. It really was no contest, as Seton

131

Hall won easily, 92—73, to win their first Big East regular season championship outright.

Danny came off the bench and contributed to Seton Hall's victory, their eighth straight, sending them into the Big East tournament not only with the No. 1 seed, but with a record of 24—6 and on a roll.

But this day belonged to Terry Dehere, who always seemed to play his best against St. John's. In their first meeting this season, Terry scored 41, a career high. Today he scored 36, the third highest of his career, which added to his Seton Hall career record and broke another record. When he buried a three-pointer with 7:07 left in the first half, he broke St. John's Chris Mullin's Big East scoring record. They stopped the game for another brief ceremony.

Later, Terry would show the kind of grace and humility we've come to expect of him when he reminded the media that he was fortunate to break Mullin's record with the aid of the three-point shot; that if Chris had had the benefit of the three-pointer, he might have set a record that never would have been broken.

No matter what happens from here on, it's been a great season for Terry, and for Bobby. Terry was named Big East Player of the Year, he broke Seton Hall's all-time scoring record, broke the Big East scoring record, set the Big East record for the most three-pointers, and had his number retired. Bobby set the all-time NCAA assists record and had his number retired at Duke. And both Bobby and Terry figure to be first-round picks in the NBA draft. I doubt if anything like this has ever happened to two kids who graduated from the same high school in the same year.

And let me not forget another Seton Hall senior, and another St. Anthony grad, Jerry Walker. Jerry was named the Big East Defensive Player of the Year, and against St. John's he scored his 1,000th point. That made him only the 12th player in Seton Hall history to score 1,000 points and grab 600 rebounds in their careers.

Jerry is winding up an excellent career as an extremely productive player for Seton Hall. Jerry is what basketball coaches like to call a "lunch pail" player, a guy who has a great work ethic. He might not make headlines and he might not set records and he might not dazzle you out of your seat, but you can count on him to show up every day and do his job. Coaches appreciate everything he does. Just a solid, dependable, workmanlike player. Every successful team needs a Jerry Walker; a leader, a hard worker, and someone who's willing to let the other guy get the glory.

Jerry is going to play somewhere next season. I think he can be a good addition to any NBA team. If it's not the NBA, then he'll play in Europe, and he'll make some money.

It's very fulfilling and rewarding for me to see the success of all the St. Anthony kids. What makes it so rewarding is that in my everyday job as a probation officer, I see so much negativism and failure. I come in contact with so many people who have messed up their lives, so many who could have had the success of a Terry Dehere or a Jerry Walker or a Rodrick Rhodes if only they had taken the right path in life or had the proper supervision, upbringing, and role models.

It's the nature of my job that I regularly come in contact with guys who are dying of the AIDS virus. The years of intravenous drug use is finally catching up to people. Hardly a week goes by when I don't pick up the newspaper and read about someone I know getting killed or involved in a killing. There have been four or five men on probation who, in the last year, have been murdered on the street. At the same time, I probably have another four or five who have been arrested for murder. I think it can all be traced today to crack cocaine and what happens to people because of their need for it.

You can only hope you will make a difference. You certainly try to make a difference, but in this job you can't win them all.

Your success rate is not very high. It's hard to live with that fact, but you try.

What's the success rate in any segment of society? Take five celebrities who get hooked on drugs. How many of them beat it? One out of five? Two? And in the ghetto, the percentages of success are even lower.

When I first started this job, there was a special division devoted only to drug offenders. Now, there's a special division devoted only to nondrug offenders. That's how much things have changed in a little over twenty years.

When a case comes to me, he comes with a "jacket," his criminal record. How do you start the rehabilitation process? The first problem you have to address is the addiction. Unless the addiction is under control, how can they be rehabilitated? They need a job, but if they get a job, the first thing they do with their first paycheck is buy drugs. So, if the addiction is still there, there's no hope.

Getting them jobs is not easy. I'll send 50 men out for a job and maybe one will be hired. How many employers want to take a chance with someone who has a criminal record? So I call in favors and I put my reputation on the line because I believe this guy or that guy is making a sincere effort to kick his habit and rehabilitate his life.

A major part of my job, in addition to doing adult supervision, is educating young people about the dangers of drugs, because that's where it starts, in the schools at a very early age. And that's where you can attack it. I supervise 175 to 200 adults with substance-abuse problems and once a week I go into the Jersey City public school system and other county grammar schools and I do drug-education lectures.

I usually talk to seventh and eighth grade classes because that's the age when kids are most vulnerable and most impressionable. Since most of them know who I am or know about St. Anthony's basketball program, especially the boys, I'll tie together education information about drugs and basketball and put together something that lasts about an hour and a half to two hours.

Because I know the neighborhoods so well, my talk will be related to kids from that neighborhood who I think these kids can identify with; youngsters who have taken advantage of a talent, such as basketball or baseball or track, and used that talent to continue to go through school, because the answer for all these young kids in an urban situation, I believe, is education. If you realize the importance of education, and you get it, that's something that's going to enhance your adult life.

When I give my talks at the schools, I'll bring a tape along related to how kids handle pressure, and related to school. After I'm done, I'll open the floor to questions and we'll talk about everything under the sun, anything they want to talk about. The boys want to talk about basketball. The girls may have questions about what they see on the street.

A lot of these kids are very knowledgeable. They see transactions on the street all the time. They see the kids or the young adults in the neighborhood, who seem to have a lot of money, fancy cars, and fancy clothes, things that are likely to turn a kid's head. These are the kids who are dealing drugs.

What I try to do is portray these people as they are, people who are one step from the man tapping them on the shoulder and ending their financial windfall, or the magic carpet ride they're on. They're riding high right now but it's going to end because they're going to be tapped on the shoulder by the man, they're going to be caught in surveillance, or one of their competitors is going to drop a dime on them; someone is going to be arrested and he's going to make a deal to try to save his skin by turning information over to the police that will get his competitor busted.

That's the world they live in, yet these kids see these people wearing new sweatsuits, new sneakers, or driving around in drug cars, and for a kid who doesn't understand, that might be a person who's successful. My job is to try to dispel the myth of their true success, and at the same time, try to convey the misery that's being spread and what addiction is. They are told that addiction can be someone they know who can't stop smoking cigarettes, or somebody who needs a cup of coffee in the morning to get their day started, like so many adults do.

Or how addiction can just be having a pocketful of quarters and wanting to go either to a jukebox or video game and keep popping in quarters instead of spending time with their families.

Then I'll talk about how drug addiction takes over your life, saps your potential, forces you to become antisocial and causes you to begin getting involved in illegal activities. I talk to them about negative role models, like Roy Tarpley or Sly from Sly and the Family Stone, or Marion Berry, the Mayor of Washington, D.C. I tell them that drugs don't discriminate against your intelligence, your creed, your race. If you try drugs, they're going to take over your life.

In the end, all I can hope when I give these talks is that I'm not talking to another Roy Tarpley, I'm talking to another Terry Dehere, or another Jerry Walker.

Sunday, March 7

The news wasn't as good from down South today as it was from up North yesterday. Duke played North Carolina, the nation's No. 1 team, in Chapel Hill and was blown away by the Tar Heels, 83—69, their ninth straight victory. North Carolina goes into the ACC tournament on a roll, as the No. 1 seed. Duke is the No. 3 seed for the tournament, but with some reason for hope.

They lost to North Carolina without Grant Hill, but Hill's return by the time the tournament begins should give them a shot in the arm. As a coach, it's easier to get your message across to your players when you have been blown out by 14 points than it is if you beat a team by 14. You don't have to do too much of a selling job on a team that's lost by 14. Any coach will tell you it's easier to get a team up than it is to bring a team down.

Monday, March 8

Sometimes, there's such a thing as a team being too high, too fired up, that it affects their play, as we found out tonight. This was our big game of the season, the one our guys have been waiting for all year.

We were matched against Marist of Bayonne in the Jersey City Armory in the Parochial B North Jersey semifinals. Marist beat us by 15 last year in our division finals, ending our streak of nine straight state division championships, and they were coming in a hot team, with 12 straight wins.

In addition to that, Marist is located only a few miles from St. Anthony. The kids on both teams all know one another. They play against each other in the summer playgrounds, many of them went to the same grammar schools, and they've played against each other in high school for three and four years.

It was a game that caught the interest of the entire area, a rematch of last year's division championship game that paired the teams regarded as the two best in the division. Tickets were sold out in advance. The place was jammed with more than 800 fans, all the law will allow. Several of our alumni came for the game, including Terry Dehere, Jerry Walker, and Danny. And P.J. Carlesimo showed up.

That alone would make the players uptight and suggest to them that this was more than just a high school basketball game. There was a lot more at stake than moving on to the state finals, and it showed in the way we played.

We started off all right, scoring the first time we touched the ball on an alley-oop pass and a slam by Jamar Curry. We led 11—7 after the first quarter and I was pretty confident that we were in good shape. Then we hit a cold spell.

At the half, we were down by six. That deficit grew to nine, 22—13, with 4:59 left in the third quarter. We were in deep trouble. We had gone eight minutes and 51 seconds without scoring. During that stretch, Marist scored 15 unanswered points, and at one point we made only one of 18 shots from the field. In the first half, Jalil Roberts, our best shooter, was 0-for-8 from the floor. And we lost our big guy, Roshown McLeod, with two fouls. I'm a two-fouls-and-out guy. I want him out of there so he can play the second half, but when Roshown is out, it affects Jalil. We were one and out with almost every possession and our shot selection was not good.

It's always hard to tell if the defense is good, or if circumstances and pressure cause the offense to bog down. In this case, I'm inclined to believe it was great defense, because when you have neighborhood guys who know each other as well as these guys do, then defense is going to dominate the game.

I told my players at halftime not to try to get it back all at once, but to try to get it back in pieces, a little at a time. And that's what we did after we broke our scoreless drought on a foul shot by Roshown. Our shooting began to pick up and we forced some turnovers and began to cut into their lead.

With four minutes left in the game, we had the deficit down to five, 32—27. Then Jalil hit a big 3. Marist made a foul shot, then Halim came up with a big steal. He missed the layup, but Jamar rebounded it and we were down by one, 33—32.

They scored on a jumper to make it 35—32, then Billy Lovett came through with a big, clutch play, a drive down the left side to make it 35—34. There was two minutes and four seconds left. The Jersey City Armory was going wild. You could hardly hear yourself think. Even though it was our home court, because the two schools are so close to each other, the fans were mixed and there seemed to be almost as many rooting for Marist as there were for St. Anthony.

In the next two minutes, neither team scored. Great defense, or nervousness, caused missed shots and turnovers, until Carlos Cueto and Roshown went on a two-on-one break and Carlos scored a layup with five seconds left that put us ahead, 36—35, our first lead since early in the second quarter.

Marist had a chance to take the lead when we fouled Randy Encarnacion, but he missed the first of his one-and-one. Donnell Williams, who will play for Seton Hall next season, got the rebound for them, but his shot missed and Billy Lovett grabbed the rebound and was fouled with two seconds left. Billy converted the front end of his one-and-one to make it 37—35. But he missed the second. Williams grabbed the rebound for Marist and all he could do was try a desperation, long heave at the basket, 70 feet away. My heart was in my mouth as the ball banked off the glass just to the right of the rim as the buzzer sounded. We had dodged a bullet and won, 37—35, and were on our way to our 10th division championship game in 11 years.

I was proud of my guys, and I told them so. I told them they showed me a lot of character in the game, being down by nine in the second half. They could have cracked, but they didn't. I also told them they still had a lot of work to do.

Wednesday, March 10

Our division championship game was against Essex Catholic on a neutral site, Wayne Valley High School in Wayne, N.J. We had scrimmaged Essex Catholic before the season and beat them by a large margin, which gave me something to use in our preparation for the game and in my pregame talk with my kids. I reminded them that Essex Catholic was greatly improved since we saw them, that they had great size and that a victory in a scrimmage, even by a wide margin, is not very conclusive.

I wasn't worried that my players would take Essex Catholic lightly. What did concern me was whether the tough semifinal game against Marist had taken too much out of us, or that my kids would have a letdown after pointing for that game against a neighborhood team all season long. I pounded away during practice and in my pregame talk that we hadn't accomplished anything yet and that we didn't want our season to end here. My worst fears were eased right away. We started off the game with our usual alley-oop pass and slam dunk by Jamar Curry and just went on from there.

There were a few scary moments when Essex Catholic scored five straight points and led, 5—2, but I could tell my kids were ready to play. At that point, we went on a 30—2 run, including 19 in a row, and led, 32—8, with 3:51 to play in the first half. At halftime, we were ahead, 39—14.

We probably could have won by 50 the way we were playing, but I emptied the bench and got everybody in the game and we won, 64—36. It was a clinic. We played about as well as we can play. When you have seven kids participate in major minutes in the game and feel that all seven of them played well, that's an extraordinary accomplishment.

Their focus was exceptional and their defense was tenacious. Their effort was a reflection of the year of effort by all the coaches of St. Anthony—my varsity assistants George Canda, Tom Cusick, and Jim Morley; jayvee coaches Hassan Abdullah and Greg Hall; freshman coach Gary Pitchford—and the kids who returned from last year's team. We looked at ourselves in the mirror last year after we lost in the North Jersey finals. I don't think we were disappointed in having lost as much as we were in the way we played. Losing is never too disappointing if you can say to yourself you played well and did whatever you had to do to win. We felt that all the players who came back would have real motivation, and we were right.

Jalil Roberts rediscovered his shooting touch and scored 17 points, including a three-pointer. Jamar Curry had 14, Halim Abdullah 10, Roshown McLeod and Billy Lovett seven apiece, Carlos Cueto five and Lonce Bethea four. Balanced scoring, which is what you like to see as a coach.

But it was our defense that excelled. Rashaan Palmer, who is 6—5, was the guy we felt we had to stop. He had scored 47 and 31 in two playoff games coming in and we knew we couldn't let him run wild on us. I assigned Jamar to cover him and put pressure on their guards so they didn't have a lot of good looks at him. When they did, all our other guys loaded up on him. Palmer scored seven points, only one field goal.

We were moving on. Our next game would be against St. Augustine's Prep of Richland, a chance to win our 10th State Division Championship in 11 years, our 12th in 14 years.

Friday, March 12

Seton Hall and Duke both began their conference tournaments today, Seton Hall in the Big East against Georgetown in the afternoon at Madison Square Garden; Duke in the ACC against Georgia Tech at night.

We learned last night that Bobby was named to the Associated Press all-America team along with Calbert Cheaney of Indiana, Jamal Mashburn of Kentucky, Anfernee Hardaway of Memphis State, and Chris Webber of Michigan. Terry Dehere was named to the second team all-America.

My mother called me all excited because she read in a magazine that Bobby was named one of the 100 most prominent Irish—Americans. That really made her happy, especially since I think the other 99 people on the list are all over 40.

• • •

The Seton Hall—Georgetown game was a cat fight. Knowing they were overmatched, Georgetown played rough house against Seton Hall, trying to intimidate Seton Hall by being physical. They beat up on Terry. He was pushed, elbowed, and twice, when he was driving for layups, was knocked to the floor, which I thought was a little excessive. Terry still scored 23 points and Seton Hall's talent was too much for Georgetown. Final score: Seton Hall 83, Georgetown 69.

• • •

Danny: That's just Georgetown. It's typical of them. They play hard. They tried to do what they had to do to win. John Thompson is a great coach. He knew his team was overmatched, so he was just trying to get us out of our normal game. He was trying to play head games with us. I didn't think it was dirty, just hard, aggressive basketball. Just a team doing what they thought it would take to win the game.

· · ·

Danny played 17 minutes and made a significant contribution to the win. He scored 10 points on two-for-two from the floor and five-for-six from the foul line. He grabbed four rebounds, had two assists, and when Georgetown had rallied to tie at 49-all, Danny had a three-pointer in a 9—2 run that helped Seton Hall start to pull away.

It was a different story that night in Charlotte, when Georgia Tech beat Duke, 69—66, knocking Duke out of the ACC tournament. Bobby played well. He scored 17 points, had eight assists, two steals, and no turnovers. But Grant Hill, in his first game back after that toe injury, didn't contribute much.

Losing in the first round of the ACC could be a blessing in disguise for Duke. That tournament requires three games in three days and might have been too much for Hill. By losing in the first round, it would give his injured toe more time to heal. On the other hand, Duke has to be concerned about Grant getting back in sync with the rest of the guys. That's where the early rounds of the NCAA tournament will help.

· · ·

Bobby: Losing this game hurt for two reasons. For one, it was the first time in my four years that Duke didn't win the ACC tournament and that was hard to take. It was a pride factor.

More important, we needed to get Grant Hill more games.

His toe was completely healed, but he was not in game shape. We needed to win this game and play a few more in the tournament to get Grant sharp. We needed the guys around him to get used to playing with him again. This was going to be important when we started the NCAA tournament.

. . .

I think anyone would be foolish to count Duke out of the NCAA tournament. In the last three years, they're 17—1 in the tournament and, as Coach K pointed out, they reached the final game in each of the last three years and in only one of those years did they win the ACC tournament.

Saturday, March 13

Seton Hall made it to the finals of the Big East tournament by beating Providence, which proved to be a very stubborn opponent. Seton Hall led by 11 at the half, but every time they would draw out to a big lead and it looked like the game was in hand, Providence just kept coming back. But every time Providence came back and got it down to five points, Seton Hall would put on a spurt and build its lead back up.

Seton Hall's lead was only five with a little more than five minutes left. Providence was hanging on, and coming on. In the next two and a half minutes, Terry Dehere buried two 3s and scored on a drive down the foul lane and Seton Hall won, 69—60. Terry scored 28 points. Danny played 23 minutes, missed his three shots from the field, made five-of-six from the foul line, but his biggest contribution was a game high seven assists. Another meaningful contribution for Danny. And Seton Hall was in the championship game of the tournament against Syracuse, a team that is on NCAA probation. So you knew the Orangemen would be motivated for the final game because it would be their last game of the season.

Sunday, March 14

The final score tells it all. Seton Hall 103, Syracuse 70. And if that's not enough, consider this. The 103 points are the most ever scored in the Big East tournament final game. The 33-point margin of victory was the largest ever in a Big East final. The defeat was the worst ever suffered by a Jim Boeheim-coached team and only the second time a Boeheim team had allowed 100 points, and that's in almost 600 games.

It was total destruction, a dominant and near-perfect game for Seton Hall. They took the early lead, led by 14 at the half and by 30 with 10 minutes left. They made 60 percent of their shots from the field, were 10-for-20 from three-point range, had 25 assists and held Syracuse to 39 percent from the field.

And they got balanced scoring. Twelve guys scored, four of them in double figures—Arturas Karnishovas 20, Jerry Walker 19, Terry Dehere 17, Luther Wright 14. Again, Danny led Seton Hall with seven assists. Terry Dehere was named Most Valuable Player of the tournament.

The only anxious moments Seton Hall had were when Luther Wright fell and twisted his left ankle and when Bryan Caver collided with Conrad McRae and twisted his left knee. Luther went out, then came right back in and was all right. But Bryan, who plays ahead of Danny at point guard, limped off the court with about seven minutes left in the first half and didn't come back until the second half. Then, with the game well in hand, P.J. Carlesimo took Bryan out with about 17 minutes left in the game and kept him out. He should be all right for the NCAAs.

Seton Hall has peaked at exactly the right time. They've won

11 straight going into the NCAA tournament to finish with a record of 27—6. They have an intimidating big man in 7—2 Luther Wright and a hot shooter in Terry Dehere. They play excellent defense and because of Bryan Caver's injury, and so many one-sided games, P.J. has a bench that has contributed and has gained some experience. He has nine players who have played quite a bit this season and who have done well, and in a (potentially) six games-in-19 days tournament, it's important to have depth.

• • •

With the Seton Hall game over, we had to wait about four hours for the NCAA to announce the draw for the big tournament. It came at 6:30 P.M., and I was pleased with the way it broke down.

Seton Hall was placed in the Southeast region as the No. 2 seed and will play Tennessee State in the first round at Orlando. Then they would play the winner of Western Kentucky vs. Memphis State. If they survive the second round, they go to the regionals in Charlotte, where they could conceivably meet Kentucky in the regional finals, the last step before the Final Four. A Seton Hall—Kentucky matchup would have particular interest for St. Anthony because it would mean Danny, Jerry Walker, and Terry Dehere, all St. Anthony kids, against another St. Anthony alumnus, Rodrick Rhodes, a freshman at Kentucky.

Duke was given a No. 3 seed in the Midwest region and they play their first game against Southern Illinois in Chicago. After that, they would play the winner of California vs. LSU. If they survive the second round, it's on to St. Louis for the regionals, where Duke could hook up with the No. 1 seed and No. 1 team in the country, Indiana.

When the draw was announced, what I was looking for was

147

when Duke would meet Seton Hall, provided they both keep winning. And that wouldn't happen until the championship game in New Orleans on Monday, April 5.

I could live with that.

Tuesday, March 16

On Sunday, February 7, we played St. Augustine Prep of Richland, N.J., in their gym and beat them, 81 –55. I emptied my bench. All 18 players got into the game and 12 of them scored, so we could have beaten them worse than that.

Now we were playing them for the New Jersey Parochial B state championship and, right away, I'm sure you can see my main concern. When you beat a team by 26 points in the regular season, then face them for a state championship, you also face a major problem. You know your opponent is going to be supremely motivated because they want to avenge that first loss. Always on the high school level, where you're dealing with players who are emotionally immature, when there's a blowout in the first meeting, the team that got blown out will concentrate more in the second meeting, and the team that did the blowing out will concentrate less.

It was up to me to make sure my kids maintained their concentration and didn't take St. Augustine's lightly. I did this by emphasizing not so much the opponent, but the importance of this game, reminding the older guys how miserable they felt last year when we lost our division championship, and by reinforcing how proud they would feel to be able to call themselves state champs.

I had another problem. This game was originally scheduled for last Saturday, but had to be postponed until tonight because we were hit with one of the biggest snowstorms of the century. More than two feet of snow was dumped on the New York—New Jersey area making travel nearly impossible and certainly very dangerous.

I worried that the layoff would hurt us because the kids were ready to play three nights ago. Would they be ready tonight? We couldn't do anything on Saturday. On Sunday, we had practice for whatever kids could get there. Nine showed up and we worked on our halfcourt game. We had a full practice on Monday, but our schedule was disjointed. I tried to combat this by making our one full practice very vigorous and spirited, simulating game conditions as best as I could.

The game was played at Elizabeth High School, a neutral site. The kids went to the game by bus from St. Anthony, but Chris, Melissa, and I drove from home, which is my usual routine. I never travel on the team bus. It's just a habit of mine, and a small superstition.

The stands were a little more than half filled, about 1,200, which I'm not proud to admit because New Jersey high school basketball is about as good as any in the country and a state championship game deserves better attendance. One reason is that all the other state divisional finals were being played on the same night. Another factor is that when you have a student body of 276, you're not going to be able to fill up any gym with your students.

To be honest, I was somewhat surprised by what happened when the game started. High school basketball in New Jersey is played in four eight-minute quarters and St. Augustine didn't score a point until there was one second left to play in the first quarter. Not one.

It wasn't that our defense was that good. St. Augustine wasn't trying to score. They had come out with the intention of stalling, slowing down the game. St. Augustine's coach, Paul Rodio, obviously figured the only way his team had a chance to win was by holding the ball and shortening the game.

They had no starter taller than 6—3, so they knew they had to keep our 6—8 center, Roshown McLeod, off the boards. They knew they couldn't rebound with us or run with us, so they tried this tactic. They thought it could get us out of sync, frustrate us, and cause us to be anxious, and it worked. For a half.

They took only three shots in the first seven minutes and 59 seconds and missed them all. They kept the ball outside on the perimeter, just tossing it back and forth. Occasionally, but not very often, they moved in for a shot, but they shot only seven-foot jumpers and layups.

We scored three baskets on steals and layups and led, 6—0, until they scored with one second left in the first quarter on a driving layup. The St. Augustine player was fouled, made the shot, and the score after one quarter was 6—3.

I think my kids were a little rattled by what St. Augustine's was doing. It's their basic instinct to run and jump and push the ball up the court, and play aggressive defense. I could sense their frustration and anxiety, especially on offense. Our shot selection hadn't been very good.

The pattern continued in the second period and at halftime, the score was 11—11.

I had a slight inkling that something like this was going to happen, but not to the extent it did. One of my assistant coaches had scouted St. Augustine in their division championship game. After the game, he talked with Coach Rodio, who said, "I've got to do something to disrupt your guys and take them out of their game."

I had told my kids they had to be ready, that St. Augustine might slow down the game, but I never dreamed they'd try to do it for as long as they did. It's the first time it's ever happened to me. I think if we had scored two or three quick baskets, it might have got them out of the stall, but when the score was only 6—0 late in the first period, it encouraged them to keep it up.

What Rodio did is within the rules. There is no shot clock in New Jersey high school basketball, but watching this kind of slowdown game is about as exciting as watching grass grow. The NBA became an exciting and viable major sport when they adopted the 24-second clock. Even the college game boomed with the 45-second shot clock.

There has been some sentiment for a shot clock in high school basketball and I'm in favor of it. But while it would be good for the game, it isn't practical because there aren't enough competent people available to run a shot clock. It's sometimes tough enough getting competent people as scorers and game timers for regular season games. And the suggestion that you can have a shot clock just for championship games is not the solution because you don't want to play the game under two sets of rules, one for the regular season and another for championships and tournaments.

I could understand what Rodio was doing. To him, it was a strategy to try to win. He felt shortening the game was his only chance and he took advantage of the rules. There's nothing illegal with that but I would never do it, especially in a championship game. I think it takes the game away from the players and it sends a message to your team that you don't believe you can beat your opponent unless you bend the rules in your favor.

Another problem is that to play this kind of game expends a lot of energy and your team has nothing left at the end. Every possession becomes critical. The reason it worked as long as it did was because when we got possession we tried too hard to get the ball to our big guys, Roshown and Jalil. Panic set in and when that happens, you take bad shots.

What I was watching reminded me of stories I had heard about the semifinals of the New York City Public High Schools championship about 30 years ago. Boys High School in Brooklyn, which had a great reputation in the '50s and '60s with players like Sihugo Green, Lenny Wilkens, and Tommy Davis, had a powerhouse team, led by Connie Hawkins, who is a legend on the playgrounds and in the high school gyms of New York City.

Boys High played against Columbus High School of the Bronx, which was coached by Roy Rubin, who later coached at LIU and Philadelphia in the NBA. Rubin decided he couldn't beat Boys playing normal basketball, so he slowed down the tempo and held onto the ball. The score was something like 12—4 at the half, and ended with Boys High winning by about 22—14. They still talk about that game more than 30 years later. Maybe 30 years from now, they'll be talking about St. Anthony vs. St. Augustine.

During intermission, I told my players not to be afraid, to take some chances. They were not going to make any effort to shoot the ball, so if we attacked them, took some chances, gambled, we could take them out of their game. So we put pressure on the ball, double and triple-teamed it, and we got some steals. I also made a "brilliant" coaching move.

That brilliant move was putting Billy Lovett in for Halim Abdullah after Halim collided with a St. Augustine's player and got his bell rung. Billy was going to play a lot anyway, but I hadn't planned to use him at this particular time. And it was Billy Lovett, coming off our bench, who turned the game around.

Billy hit a short jumper from the paint to put us ahead, 15—13, then he made two consecutive steals and scored layups after each. On one of his layups, he was fouled and hit the shot. So he had scored seven points in 20 seconds to put us ahead, 20—13.

We pressed our advantage and Billy never let up. He scored

six points on a 12—0 run that put us up, 23—13. Billy also did a super job on defense, not only picking them up at halfcourt and getting those quick steals that gave us a chance to score without taking time off the clock, but holding their all-Atlantic County guard, Matt Miles, to four points in the second half, after he had scored eight in the first half.

As I said before, when you get a lead on a team that is stalling, the clock becomes their enemy and our ally. Now they were forced to put the ball up and our size advantage and fast break took command of the game. With three and a half minutes left, we were ahead, 41—19, which means we had outscored them, 30—8, in 11 minutes. At that point, it was time for me to empty my bench, my version of the Red Auerbach victory cigar. The final score was 55—27, so even our subs outscored them, 14—8. I got 13 kids into the game and 10 of them scored.

Billy Lovett ended up our high scorer with 16 points and was named the Most Valuable Player of the game, which is unusual for a junior, but even more unusual for a "bench" player. I really don't think of Billy as a sub. I call him my sixth starter. As Red Auerbach once said, it's not important who starts a game, it's important who finishes it, and Billy Lovett has been in there at the end of a lot of games. He plays as many minutes as any of our five starters. He's been the first one off the bench for us all year and I have no doubt he would be a starter for almost any team in the state. This is a wonderful indication of the team St. Anthony has and that it's not Roshown McLeod or Jalil Roberts, but a sum of all the parts. On a night when Jalil wasn't getting the ball and scored only two points, Billy Lovett stepped up and did the job for us.

I'm very proud of Billy. He's a wonderful kid. He made a commitment to St. Anthony by coming to Jersey City from East Orange, taking a bus and a train every day to get to school. He's also an excellent student, so he has a chance to have an outstanding college career. I think he's a big-time college point guard.

. . .

We had won our 10th Parochial B state championship in the last 11 years, our 12th in the last 14 years, and we were going to the Tournament of Champions, where the six state champs, four from the public schools, and two from the parochial schools, will meet for the overall state championship.

I was shocked to learn that Shawnee from Medford, N.J., which had won the Tournament of Champions last season, had been beaten in its championship game and would not be going to the Tournament of Champions. Shawnee was No. 1 in the state and we were No. 2. Shawnee was No. 4 in the country in the *USA Today* poll and we were No. 7. I know the players and coaches of Shawnee were disappointed that they would not get a chance to defend their title, and I felt for them. I also know that the people who follow New Jersey high school basketball were looking forward to a Shawnee—St. Anthony matchup. But I have to be honest. A coach always looks for the easiest road to win a championship and Shawnee is a very good team. Having them out of the Tournament of Champions was not going to hurt our chances.

So this was going to be the six-team lineup for the Tournament of Champions:

From the public schools, the Group IV champion, Irvington High School, 24—1, with 2,517 students; the Group III champion, Red Bank Regional of Little Silver, 28—1, with 1,057 students; the Group II champion, Middle Township of Cape May County Court House, 28—2, with 850 students; the group I champion, Perth Amboy Tech, 23—3, with 194 students, mostly boys.

From the parochial schools, the Group A champion, Seton Hall Prep, 24—2, with 730 students, all boys; and the Group B champion, St. Anthony, 26—1, with 276 students, almost half of them girls.

Thursday, March 18

With Shawnee knocked out of the Tournament of Champions, we were given the No. 1 seed and a bye in the first round tonight. We play Saturday at Rutgers against the winner of Seton Hall Prep vs. Red Bank Regional.

Duke and Seton Hall both play their first round games in the NCAA tournament tonight, Duke against Southern Illinois in the Midwest Region in Chicago at 8:00 P.M.; Seton Hall against Tennessee State in the Southeast Region in Orlando at 10.

I was going to have to scout the Seton Hall Prep—Red Bank game, so I would miss the Duke game, although I would try to find a television and sneak peeks when I could. I hoped to get home in time to watch Seton Hall—Tennessee State.

I have had a chance to digest the NCAA draw since it first came out. I think it's a good draw for Seton Hall, until they get to the Regionals where they might have to play Florida State and Kentucky. That's two tough games in three days, but the way Seton Hall is playing right now, I like their chances of getting to the Final Four.

Duke has a tougher draw. If they beat Southern Illinois, they probably would get California, a very good team, in the second round. After that, they would face the possibility of two tough games in the Regionals, Kansas and Indiana.

Since the draw, I've been getting calls from a lot of people who say they're in office pools and in their draw, it comes up Seton Hall against Duke for the championship game. Wouldn't that be something, Seton Hall against Duke, Bobby against Danny, in New Orleans?

One friend, Bobby Hahner, even said he had a dream about the NCAA tournament. In his dream, Bobby said, Seton Hall meets Duke for the championship on April 5. The score is tied with just a few seconds left on the clock. Danny has the ball. He's being guarded by Bobby. Danny goes up for a jump shot. Bobby goes up with him. Danny gets the shot off. It goes in. And Seton Hall wins the national championship.

Because of our St. Anthony games, I won't get to see the NCAA tournament until the Regionals. We have our plans all set. Chris will go to St. Louis to see Duke. I will go to Charlotte to see Seton Hall. And then we meet up, hopefully, in New Orleans for the Final Four.

· · ·

Duke lost its last two games before the tournament, so a lot of people were counting them out in their try for a third straight NCAA championship. But I was confident, especially with Grant Hill back at almost 100 percent. Southern Illinois would be a good test for them, though not a serious threat. What I think Duke had to do, as defending national champions, was show a little arrogance on the court, a little smugness. They had to project an attitude of "We're the champs and you're going to have to knock us off."

Mike Krzyzewski is right when he said the way Duke finished

158

the regular season was irrelevant. "You forget about all that," he said. "You focus on now."

Bobby told me he had personally called a meeting and chastised the team for their lack of intensity toward the end of the season. I wonder where he learned how to do that? He said he felt, as the senior point guard, it was his duty to try to rally the team for the tournament. For three years, Bobby was beat on by Christian Laettner, who never hesitated to let his teammates know when he thought they were not doing their jobs.

In last year's championship game against Michigan, Bobby turned the tables on Christian during halftime. Laettner had only two baskets and two rebounds and seven turnovers and Duke trailed by one. Bobby didn't address his remarks to Lateener directly, but told the team in general that they were blowing it. He urged them to come out in the second half and perform or see their second straight national championship slip away. While he didn't talk directly to Laettner, he didn't have to. Everybody knew who Bobby had in mind.

· · ·

Bobby: A lot of people misunderstood my relationship with Christian Laettner. We weren't the best of friends, but we were united in the common goal of trying to win a national championship. Who says you have to be the best friend of your teammate? You can't be close to all of them. The important thing is that you have mutual respect and that you work together toward the same goal. I respected Christian as a guy who wanted to win, and I like to think he felt the same way about me.

· · ·

For someone to be a true leader, he has to do it with deeds as well as words. In last year's title game, Bobby did it by looking for Laettner and getting him the ball. Christian ended with 19 points and seven rebounds and Duke outscored Michigan in the second half, 41—20, for a 71—51 victory and their second consecutive national championship.

Now Bobby was going to have to do it again. He was going to have to get his team pumped for the NCAA tournament. And it was going to have to start right now, in the first game against Southern Illinois.

· · ·

Bobby: The way I looked at it, the Southern Illinois game was do or die. If we lose, we're out. I didn't want that and I was going to do everything I could to prevent that from happening. I figured if I stepped up and played well, and played confidently, the rest of the guys would respond to that and play up to that level.

· · ·

Against Southern Illinois, Bobby did it all. He passed and he shot. He had seven assists and led Duke with 25 points on eight-of-nine from the field, including six-for-seven on three-point shots. It was obvious he had made a personal commitment to be Duke's leader and to try to carry the team on his back through the tournament, to the Final Four.

Duke put on an offensive clinic against Southern Illinois. At one point, they made 10 straight shots from the field. They rolled to a 105—70 victory, their 13th straight in the NCAA tournament, which served notice on the rest of the field that the Blue Devils were back in gear and would have to be reckoned with for the rest of the tournament.

I was feeling much better about Duke's chances after that first game. What made me feel good was the way Duke played, the way they went about their business, with confidence, and the kind of arrogance that all winners have. They were saying.

"We're the champs and you're going to have to take that title away from us."

In their second-round game, Duke was going to draw a tough opponent, California, which had beaten LSU by two points in the first round. The newspapers already were billing it as a head-to-head showdown between Bobby and California's sensational freshman point guard, Jason Kidd.

. . .

If Duke was awesome on offense against Southern Illinois in the first round, Seton Hall was awesome on defense against Tennessee State in their first round game. And there was nothing wrong with Seton Hall's offense, either.

Seton Hall shot 46 percent from the field, 83 percent from the free throw line and 53 percent from three-point range, while holding Tennessee State to 35 percent from the field and 24 percent from three-point range and rolled to an 81—59 victory. Terry Dehere had 19 points, six assists and four rebounds. Danny had nine points with three-out-of-four from three-point range, one assist and one turnover in 22 minutes. P.J. Carlesimo used 12 players and 10 of them scored as Seton Hall won its 12th straight and did nothing to change my mind that this is a Final Four team.

. . .

Danny: I was really feeling good about our team after the Tennessee State game. We just kicked their butts. It seemed to carry over from the Syracuse game for the Big East tournament championship. Everybody played hard. Luther Wright got in foul trouble, but it didn't seem to matter. We were completely in control of the game. The way we played, I just felt like we were on a roll and we had everything going right. We really believed we could beat any team in the country.

· · ·

In the second round, Seton Hall would meet Western Kentucky. I was feeling pretty good about both Bobby and Danny advancing to the Sweet Sixteen.

Saturday, March 20

A big day for the Hurleys. Three games to be concerned about, to draw our attention. And the timing couldn't be much better.

At 3:00 P.M., we were scheduled to play Seton Hall Prep in the semifinals of the Tournament of Champions. Seton Hall Prep had beaten Red Bank Regional in the preliminary round.

Our game should end around 4:30. In the NCAA tournament, Seton Hall University was playing Western Kentucky at 4:45. Our game was at the Rutgers University gym in Piscataway, which is about a half-hour drive from Jersey City. So, we would listen to the first half of Seton Hall—Western Kentucky on the car radio, then get home in time to watch the second half on television. That would be followed, almost immediately, by Duke against California at 7:00.

First things first. Bob Farrell's Seton Hall Prep team is a good one, with a record of 25—2, They had won the Parochial A state championship for the third straight year. So the winner of our

ne would, in effect, be the parochial school champion of the
ntire state of New Jersey.

Seton Hall had a veteran team led by 5—10 guard Brevin
Knight, whose father, Mel, had been an outstanding player at
Seton Hall University. Brevin Knight was clearly the best guard in
the state and one of the best players we would face all season. He
is quick and has great moves and was signed to go to Stanford, so
that tells you that in addition to being an excellent player, he's
very intelligent. Our job was to try to control Knight and keep
him from going wild and, because Seton Hall is not very big, to
win the battle off the boards and try to get the ball to Roshown
McLeod down low.

We scored the first eight points of the game, stretched our
lead to 18—7, then to 28—12. But I wasn't fooled by our fast
start. I knew this game wasn't going to be easy. And it wasn't.

Brevin Knight started to do what he does best, being totally
disruptive at both ends of the floor. Seton Hall scored the last
seven points of the first half and the first four of the second half
and cut our lead to 28—23. We were in a battle. And they had
the momentum.

But our kids have been able to withstand almost every challenge this season and this was no exception. It stayed close
through three quarters, 39—34, but early in the fourth quarter,
we got the ball into Roshown, who went to the hoop, scored, and
was fouled. He made the foul shot to give us an eight-point lead
and take the pressure off. But only temporarily.

Billy Lovett came off the bench to score two baskets, but
Knight got a put-back and a 3 to cut our lead to 47—41. Then
Billy Lovett went up strong for an offensive rebound, was fouled
and sank them both, and Carlos Cueto drove in for a layup and
we were home free.

The final score was 51—41. Brevin Knight ended his high
school career for Seton Hall by scoring 27 points and, believe me,
he earned every one of them. Roshown McLeod had 17 points

and seven rebounds. Jalil Roberts had 14 points. And we were in the Tournament of Champions finals for the fourth time in its five years, looking for our third championship.

Now it was into the car and on the way home to watch Danny and Bobby play on television. I almost wish I had missed it.

. . .

Chris: From the moment that little rock hit the windshield of our car and I heard it crack when we were driving to the state tournament game, I knew this was going to be a bad day. A stone came off the turnpike, hit the bottom of the windshield and I heard it. Bob was in the car, but he didn't hear a thing. He was so engrossed in his game that if a boulder came up and hit him in the head, you'd have to tell him about it.

But we won our tournament game, so I figured maybe this wouldn't be such a bad day, after all. I was wrong.

We heard part of the Seton Hall game on the car radio on the way home from the St. Anthony game. Danny was hardly playing. When we got home and turned on the TV, Danny played great. The only thing that worried me was that the coach of Western Kentucky, Ralph Willard, had been an assistant coach under Rick Pitino with the Knicks. I was afraid of that because Pitino was a really good coach.

. . .

I had bad vibes about Seton Hall right from the start, in the first half. They were turning the ball over too often, missing opportunities, and Western Kentucky was playing aggressively, with a nothing-to-lose attitude. So much had been expected of Seton Hall that it was hard to accept what I was hearing and seeing. I kept thinking, and hoping, that they would get it together in the second half, that their experience and their talent would carry them through.

And it almost did. They fought back and then Danny stepped

of the Duke game, but I couldn't tell you what happen
one of the worst days I ever experienced.

. . .

I don't scream and yell or shout and cheer when I watch a
game on television, even when my own kids are playing. I inter-
nalize. I keep everything inside. And I watch the game like a
coach. I'll get analytical watching a game and I'll offer advice to
the TV set.

A lot of people said they thought Seton Hall took Western
Kentucky too lightly, that they were looking ahead to Florida
State and then to Kentucky. I don't think that's what happened.
I think what P.J. Carlesimo said was right. He said Western Kentucky is a team that does a lot of different things, plays multiple
defenses, and Seton Hall needed more time to prepare for them.
Plus, the Seton Hall kids never even got to see Western Kentucky
on television, so they knew nothing about them. That's not an
excuse. That's not a disappointed father talking. That's a coach
trying to be objective and analytical in an effort to explain what
so many people found unexplainable.

I felt bad for Danny, but I felt even worse for Terry Dehere
and Jerry Walker. Danny is only a sophomore. He'll get a chance
to get back there again. Terry and Jerry won't. They were seniors
at St. Anthony the last time Seton Hall made the Final Four, and
got all the way to the NCAA finals against Michigan, then lost in
overtime. P.J. had been building for this team, his best shot at
the Final Four in four years, and now he was out of it. Terry
Dehere and Jerry Walker were out of it. In four years, the farthest
they had gone in the NCAA tournament was the Sweet Sixteen,
so I knew they had to be tremendously disappointed.

Terry had a great season and a great career and he has an ex-
cellent pro career ahead of him. He scored 30 points against
Western Kentucky, but he was one-for-nine on 3s and, knowing
Terry, I know he'll be blaming himself.

wanted this so badly, and he worked so hard. He's a
.rul kid and I know how much he wants to win. It had to
.ugh on him to accept losing, knowing he'll never put on a
.on Hall uniform again. At least Bobby could look back and
.eel good that he was there and he won a national championship.
Terry Dehere and Jerry Walker never did, so I was hurting for
them.

. . .

Chris: After Seton Hall lost, I was devastated. Melissa was
sitting on the couch and she said, "Oh, this is great. Now all
that has to happen is for Duke to lose." All of a sudden, I had
this feeling in the pit of my stomach, that this was not going to
go well.

. . .

Needless to say I was in a foul mood with Seton Hall losing,
but there still was the Duke game. There still was hope that one
of my boys would make it to the Final Four.

. . .

Bobby: I was warming up when I looked up and saw that
Seton Hall lost. I felt bad for Danny, Jerry, and Terry. Danny
and I had sort of kidded about playing against each other again,
this time for the NCAA championship. Now he was out of the
tournament. But I couldn't dwell on that. I had a game to play.

. . .

Even with the shock of Seton Hall, the realization that anything can happen, and you can't take anything for granted in
sports, I guess I still wasn't prepared for what came next.

Right from the start, I had a bad feeling about Duke vs. California. Duke didn't come out with the same intensity they had
against Southern Illinois. And the California kids were playing

very aggressively, hitting their 3s and playing with the abandon that suggested they had nothing to lose.

Cal had been the center of a big controversy when the versity fired Coach Lou Campanelli for supposedly abusing kids, yelling at them, demeaning them. When they replaced Campanelli with Todd Bozeman, only 29, their record was 10—7. Under Bozeman, they were 10—1, then beat LSU on a miracle buzzer-beating shot by Jason Kidd, their terrific freshman guard. Obviously, the change in coaches had loosened things up and that's the way Cal was playing against Duke, good and loose.

In addition, after California beat LSU, Dale Brown, LSU's coach made a comment that made me cringe when I read it in the papers. He obviously was a supporter of Lou Campanelli, as a lot of veterans in the college coaching fraternity were. After he was beaten by California, he had a few sour grapes. He was quoted as saying California didn't "have a prayer against Duke."

Thanks a lot coach. What he had done, inadvertently, was give California even more incentive to beat Duke. I'm not saying that's what did it, but every little bit helps. You can bet the Cal kids read that quote, and if they didn't, you can be sure Coach Bozeman pointed it out to them and the newspaper clipping wound up posted in the California dressing room.

California went up by 10 at the half and, to make matters worse, Duke's big guy, Cherokee Parks, went down late in the first half and never returned, which took away any kind of inside game they could play.

The lead got to 18 in the second half and that's when Bobby decided to take matters into his own hands. He turned from passer to scorer, which is not his game, but that's Bobby for you. He's willing to do whatever he has to do to win, and Duke needed offense. So he gave them offense. If the players on his team won't take charge, then he will. If he didn't, Duke never would have been in the game. They would have fallen behind by 30 points.

wouldn't let that happen. Almost singlehandedly, he
t them back. He made eight-of 13 goals from the field,
of-nine from three-point range. But he needed help, and he
s getting very little. I had thought that Grant Hill was all the
way back from his injury, but obviously, he wasn't. He and
Thomas Hill did get hot for a time and Duke went ahead, 77—76
with 1:11 to play.

When Duke got the lead, I figured they would put Cal away.
Basketball is very much a game of momentum, and it was obvious the momentum had swung to Duke. I thought because of
their experience and their winning history, they would surely de-
liver the knockout punch on a young and suddenly desperate
California team. But give those Cal kids credit. They didn't fold.
They came back, held Duke scoreless over the last 71 seconds,
and won, 82—77. I was stunned. I couldn't believe it.

Bobby made only one of his last nine shots, although he had
some good looks at the basket. But he was simply fatigued. He
played the entire 40 minutes, and when you're tired and your legs
are wobbly, it affects your shooting.

. . .

**Chris: Bobby was just about the only Duke player out there
killing himself. He gave it his all. If Bobby had to end his college career, he couldn't have ended it on a better personal note.
He played a great, great game. He almost won the game all by
himself. But I should have known, ever since that rock hit the
car windshield.**

. . .

Even in my disappointment and heartbreak, I was so proud of
Bobby. He played an heroic game, did everything he could to try
to help Duke win. I couldn't have been prouder of his effort, but
as television commentator Clark Kellogg correctly pointed out,
when you have to depend on your point guard as your primary

170

…my heart cry for him, and there was a shot of Jason Kidd …e of the television announcers was saying that Kidd was …eir apparent to Bobby as college basketball's premier point …ard.

Later, in the press conference, Coach K broke down and cried. I felt like joining him.

"All this talk about college sports being bad," he said. "When I hear that, I want to whack everybody who says that. College sports is great. I've been the luckiest guy in the world the last four years.

"I was clapping because I wanted to say thanks. I've had more accolades in the last seven years than any college coach, and I understand what makes a college coach. It's the kids. We didn't lose this basketball game. Cal won it."

Bobby and Thomas Hill, his two seniors, were sitting next to Coach K.

"It tears me up that we lost," Coach K said, "only because I don't have the opportunity to coach these two guys anymore. Losing a game, it doesn't mean a damn thing. I won for a long time with these guys and I'll win for the rest of my life for my association with them.

"They've taken me places and given me experiences that no college coach has had over the last 20 years. It's only sad that I can't do it anymore with them. Bobby and Thomas have been like sons to me. Bobby has had a storied career and I'm glad to have been part of the story. Tonight was an example of who he is and who he will be for whoever is fortunate enough to coach him in the future."

Coach K is down now, and I'm feeling down for him, but he can't complain. He's had a great run. Duke can't get a lot of the kids other schools can because they're a step above most of their competitors academically. And he certainly accomplished a lot in his time. But I'm sure he's wondering where he's ever going to get another kid to run his team like Bobby did.

I had had such ambitious plans. When the dr.
NCAA tournament came out and it worked out that
Hall and Duke, Danny and Bob, were going to meet, it was
to have to be in the championship game, I thought that was
good to be true. Now it won't happen.

This was Black Saturday for the Hurleys. I just sat there
stunned as first Seton Hall and then Duke was beaten. In the
span of two and a half hours, both Bobby and Danny, also Terry
Dehere and Jerry Walker, were knocked out of the NCAA tournament. I couldn't believe it. A double dagger to my heart. Chris
and I were both personally devastated by those losses. I couldn't
ever remember feeling so low.

Watching my two sons playing against each other in last
year's Regional finals was agony for me. But watching them both
lose in the second round on the same night was worse. Given the
choice, I would much prefer to have to endure the agony of seeing them playing against each other.

Sunday, March 21

I hardly slept at all last night, I was so upset with what had happened on Black Saturday. When I did drop off to a fitful sleep, I kept thinking I was going to wake up and discover it was all just a bad dream. But it wasn't.

They say you don't have to rest, that you'll get a lot of rest in your grave. The way I'm feeling today, that seems like a viable alternative.

We talked to both Bobby and Danny last night. Bobby called three times. He was having a tough time dealing with losing, because it was so abrupt. He kept saying that he still couldn't believe it, that when the game ended, he didn't know how to react. He didn't know if he should stay on the court or just walk off. He said he was a little lost for a moment. And he couldn't believe he had played his last game for Duke.

. . .

Chris: Bobby called first. It was about one or two in the morning. He was upset. He was crying. Danny called about 5:00 A.M. and he was upset.

We talked to Bobby again before we went to our game at the Meadowlands. Bobby said it was hard for him to lose that way, because he never did anything but play in the last game of the season and now there were no more games. He said he always used to wonder how he would react if he wasn't in the last game and now he knew. He said it felt horrible. And he never stopped crying.

All I could do was listen to him and try to console him as best I could.

I told him he had had a great year and a great career. Of all the players Bob has coached, Bobby is the only one who ever went to the Final Four. And Bobby made it to the NCAA championship game three times and won it twice.

. . .

Bobby also called Danny and the two of them talked for a long time, consoling each other.

. . .

Danny: We sort of took turns. I gave him the floor, then he gave me the floor. We listened to each other's complaints about our games. I couldn't believe we lost and he couldn't believe he lost. I could only imagine how he felt. I felt bad for him, but I couldn't feel too bad. After all, he had won two national championships and not many players have done that. I haven't won any . . . yet.

. . .

As bad as I felt, I couldn't lose sight of the fact that I still had a very important game to play with my St. Anthony team, and I couldn't let my players see me down and think that my head

wasn't in their game. I had to make them believe that I be
this game, against Middle Township of Cape May Co
Courthouse for the Tournament of Champions title and t
honor of being the No. 1 team in New Jersey, was the most im
portant thing on my mind.

As it turned out, I didn't have to worry about these kids, as I
would find out before the game. It's our practice to take the team
for a pregame meal to Artie's Restaurant on Henderson Street in
Jersey City. The restaurant is owned by my friends Artie
Zinicola, Rich McKeever, and Brian Doherty, and they graciously
feed the team before every game.

The pregame meal has become a tradition, a nice treat for the
guys to look forward to. If it's a school day, they get finished with
school, then they gather at the restaurant and eat. If it's a home
game, they just walk a few blocks to the Jersey City Armory. If it's
a road game, they get in the bus and take off, but Artie's Restaurant always is their last stop before they go to the game.

On this day, the pregame meal consisted of salad, ziti, garlic
bread, ice cream, and soda. It was, as it always has been, a social
gathering that helped relieve some of the pregame tension.

I never go. Sometimes my assistant coaches do, but I don't.
It's only partly superstition. I'm always nervous before a game,
and they don't need to see me that way. I wouldn't want that to
carry over to my players. They spend enough time with me as it
is. I do enough at practice, I don't need to make them nervous
before a game. It's best to leave them alone. We've prepared for
the game. I can't do any more on game day.

It's good for them to create an atmosphere to get themselves
ready to play. I'll get ready for the game in my own way.

Later, one of the owners of Artie's, Brian Doherty, told me
that Carlos Cueto had said to him, "We know Mr. and Mrs. Hurley are feeling bad about Bobby and Danny losing. We're going
to help them feel better by going out today and kicking Middle
Township's butts."

concern about the Middle Township game was having to
two games in two days. We used only six players yesterday
against Seton Hall Prep, so I was concerned that the kids were
going to be a little tired. Besides, we had a few guys who had a
touch of the flu, so I was planning to use a lot of players against
Middle Township.

I said very little in my pregame talk. No rah-rah stuff. These
kids didn't need it. I never had to tell them all year how important a game was. They knew without me having to remind them.
This is a wonderful bunch of kids. I can honestly say I've enjoyed
coaching them as much as any team I've ever had.

So I confined my talk to a little strategy. Middle Township,
which beat Irvington High School in yesterday's semifinals in
something of a surprise, is not as tall as we are, but they're bigger
and stronger than our kids. I was mainly concerned about their
junior point guard, LaMarr Greer, who's 6—5 and can shoot.
What I wanted them to do was play tough, pressure defense on
him and try to deny him the ball.

I assigned the job of guarding Greer to Halim Abdullah,
who's a very tenacious defender. But he's only 5—7, so he would
be giving away 10 inches in height. I wanted Carlos Cueto, the
off-guard, to help out with Greer and trap him. I would get
Halim out when he was showing signs of wearing down, and put
in Billy Lovett. I planned to rotate my three guards quite a bit,
trying to keep them fresh.

On offense, I wanted us to try to ram the ball into Roshown
McLeod in the low post, where he had a size advantage on his
opponent.

Then I went out to coach and let the kids do the rest. All I did
was fulfill the requirement of having an adult on the bench.

There were over 4,000 people in the Byrne Arena at the
Meadowlands for this championship game. The arena seats
about 17,000 for basketball, so the place seemed like it was
empty. Seton Hall had returned from Orlando and I was pleased

that Danny came to our game. He was still feeling down losing to Western Kentucky, but he was slowly coping with disappointment. Danny came with another Seton Hall play John Leahy, who happened to have played his high school bas ketball at Middle Township.

. . .

Danny: It was tough to go to the game the way I was feeling. We had been the hot ticket in New Jersey. So much was expected of us, and we let a lot of people down.

Still, I had to go to the game because I wanted to show my support to my family.

Some people recognized me and John and they were very good about it. They tried to console us and told us we still had a great year. That helped a lot. Seton Hall fans are good people. That helped take the sting out of losing. Just being there helped. I wasn't thinking about myself. I was thinking about my mother and father and the guys on the St. Anthony team.

. . .

I wish there were 40,000 fans at that game instead of 4,000. I wish New Jersey high school basketball drew like they do in Indiana or Kentucky, because that's how good I thought our performance was against Middle Township, and that's how proud I was of my kids.

We came out and surprised Middle Township by picking up the tempo of the game, playing at a much quicker pace than we did yesterday against Seton Hall Prep. Greer kept Middle Township in the game for the first quarter. He would end up with 22 points, but we made him work for every one of them. We led, 18—13, after one period, then outscored them by 14 in the second quarter for a 42—23 lead at halftime. Middle Township never got within 15 for the rest of the game. We won, 84—59, and had won the Tournament of Champions. It's been played

...nes and we have made the finals four times and won it
. times.

As promised, I used a lot of players. Thirteen got into the
game, but basically I went with eight. Roshown McLeod had 18
points and 12 rebounds. Jalil Roberts had 13 points and 10 rebounds. Jamar Curry scored 13. Justin Fredericks, who's a 6—4
junior and is going to be an important player for us next season,
came off the bench to score 12. Halim Abdullah had 11 points,
including three-for-four on 3s. And best of all, we had 25 assists
as a team, evenly distributed, with Cueto getting seven of them.

Roshown was named the Most Valuable Player of the tournament. He also finished the season with a St. Anthony record for
field goal percentage, just a shade under 70 percent. After the
game, I told the press that Roshown was a "poor man's Jerry
Walker," knowing that Roshown would read that and be thrilled
by it because all season I kept telling him he was nowhere near
like Jerry around the basket. I told him Jerry was a fearsome competitor who took away the lane from everybody when he played
for us. But Roshown did a nice imitation of Jerry today. By nature, he's not an assertive kid.

It annoys me when I keep reading that this St. Anthony team
is a team without a great player. I have a problem with that because I think Roshown McLeod and Jalil Roberts are outstanding
high school players who are equal to anyone in the state of New
Jersey. And they'll both be even better college players when they
get bigger and stronger and more experienced. And the other
players on the team were willing to sacrifice their individual stats
to put St. Anthony basketball first.

Sometimes Jalil gets overlooked when he doesn't score a lot
because he was our leading scorer and people expect him to get
his 18 or 20 or more every game. When he doesn't, they think he
had a bad game, but what most people don't realize is that he
almost always got our toughest defensive assignment. Today, he
was assigned to guard Stephano Anderson, who had scored 24

yesterday against Irvington. Jalil held him scoreless in the first half, when the game was still on the line.

I couldn't be prouder of any team I've coached. I never had more fun with a team. They were very relaxed during the season. We didn't have highs or lows, but were very consistent in our performance. The kids got disappointed when they didn't play well, not because of their egos, but because they thought they'd let me down. That's rare nowadays. It's unusual when kids feel they're letting down the coach. I appreciate that kind of kid. I hope I have that kind of kid for the rest of my coaching career.

We won the Tournament of Champions and that makes us the No. 1 team in the state. We finished the season 28—1, but that one loss, well there were circumstances. In a different environment, the outcome of that one game probably would have been different. As far as I'm concerned, this team was undefeated.

Yesterday was a tough day. Black Saturday. Winning today took some of the sting out of yesterday. Sunday was a much better day.

Tuesday, March 23

*U*SA *Today* came out with its final high school ratings today. St. Anthony was No. 4 in the country, behind Simon Gratz of Philadelphia, Martin Luther King of Chicago, and Mouth of Wilson of Oak Hill, Va., all of them much bigger schools than ours, all of them undefeated.

It's three days after Black Saturday and the hurt is beginning to ease a little, but not much. It's two days after our final game, and I admit I'm a little lost. No more basketball.

By now, I had expected to be making plans to go to Charlotte to see Danny and Seton Hall in the Sweet Sixteen, and Chris would be making plans to go to St. Louis to see Bobby and Duke. And we would be looking forward to getting together in New Orleans for the Final Four. But we have nowhere to go, and it feels strange.

There are some nice things to look forward to, however. We're planning to take the St. Anthony players on a trip to the Basketball Hall of Fame in Springfield, Massachusetts. We'll take them to the museum and to some nice restaurants.

Then, on May 4, Jersey City and the State Assembly is going ▸ have a day honoring Bobby and the two Seton Hall seniors, Terry Dehere and Jerry Walker, and the St. Anthony basketball team for being No. 1 in the state. Also, they're going to have an annual Bobby Hurley Award which will go to the best student-athlete in Jersey City.

What's so hard to accept is that Bobby's college career is over, that they're still playing college basketball and he isn't. Kentucky made it to the Final Four, which is some consolation. It means Rodrick Rhodes will be playing there and that makes four consecutive years St. Anthony's has had a representative in the Final Four.

This will be the first time in eight years, in his high school and college career, that Bobby will not be playing in a championship game and I know that's eating him up. But knowing Bobby and the kind of kid he is, I'd be surprised if he hasn't been back in the gym already, shooting baskets and working in the weight room.

It didn't turn out the way we wanted it to. There are a lot of things you can script, but you can't script life. But I want to forget about the negatives and dwell on the positives. Bobby had a great college career. In his four years, Duke's record was 115—25, a winning percentage of .821. He became college basketball's all-time assists leader, he was named an all-American, he played on a team that reached the NCAA championship game three times and won it twice, and he had his number retired. Not many players in the history of college basketball had a career that can match that.

As for his future, he'll be playing basketball in the NBA next year. I haven't begun to think about where he might play because it's still too early. The NBA playoffs haven't even started yet. Final standings are not set, so there's no way to project which team might take him.

Naturally, I'd like it to be close to home so I can get to some

games. New York or New Jersey would be nice. But the Nets ha
an outstanding point guard in Kenny Anderson and the Knick
probably will draft too low to get a crack at Bobby. Another team
in the East would be nice, too, but that would be selfish of me.
What's important is that Bobby go where he will be happy. To
him, that means a team where he fits in and can play a lot.

Danny still has two years left at Seton Hall and I expect them
to be productive years. I think you're going to see Danny step up
and be an important player for the school. His time has come. It's
not going to hurt him, either, that Bobby will be out of college
and Danny will no longer have to endure those comparisons to
his older brother.

I look for Danny to start next season, either as the point
guard or the No. 2 guard, the shooting position. He and Bryan
Caver can both play either position. Luther Wright, Seton Hall's
seven-foot, two-inch center, has decided to forego his senior year
and enter the NBA draft. That's a major loss for Seton Hall and it
indicates P.J. Carlesimo is going to have a smaller team that will
rely on quickness, defense, and good shooting, which suits
Danny's game fine.

As for St. Anthony next season, we're going to have a different look. It's two days after their championship game, but I'd be
surprised if those kids aren't in the gym already or in the weight
room building themselves up for next year. The AAUs are coming up and they'll be playing in those games.

I have a pretty good idea what we're going to have for next
season. Every coach does depth charts, looking two years ahead.
We're not going to be very big next year. We'll have more of a
guard-oriented team, smaller and quicker. I look for our two co-
captains, guards Billy Lovett and Carlos Cueto, to be the heart of
the team. I'll have a couple of 6—4 kids. One of them, Justin
Fredericks, played well in the Tournament of Champions final
and I hope that's a game he can build on. Another, Randy Clark,
just needs to believe in himself as much as we do.

I also have a kid named Michael Jordan. Now how can I foul ~~nings~~ things up with Michael Jordan on my team?

The bigger kids I have are multidimensional, so if you're an optimist, which I try to be, you look at them and you say we're small, but we're quick, so we'll take the other teams' big guys away from the basket with our 6—4 guys. You don't say to yourself, they're 6—4, what's going to happen when we play against bigger guys than us? I never think that way.

To some extent, I know the boys in the area who are in grammar school. There are some very good eighth graders and most of Jersey City's best eighth graders are coming to St. Anthony. We've got a very good group coming in, two or three or four of them with excellent potential. A couple of good-sized kids. A couple of good little guards. And all of them with a chance to grow, because when you look at kids in grammar school, you rarely can project how big they're going to be.

So, next year is going to be a new challenge. Every new season brings a new challenge, but that's what's so exciting about coaching high school kids. It will be my 22nd year at St. Anthony and I'm still not tired of it. It starts all over again in seven months. I can hardly wait.

EPILOGUE

THURSDAY, JULY 1

We are all ecstatic, beside ourselves with joy the way things worked out at the NBA draft, which was held last night at The Palace in Auburn Hills, Michigan, where the Detroit Pistons play their home games. I'm back home in Jersey City now, still filled with the excitement of last night, and a little bit weary.

Bobby has been on a whirlwind the past few weeks. Even before the draft, he signed a deal with Upper Deck, which will produce his basketball card. Then he agreed in principal on a deal with Foot Locker, which is going to use him as spokesperson for a new line of sneakers called ITZ—In The Zone. That will be for two years. After that, they will evaluate where he is and where they're going and there is the possibility of another new line of sneakers with Bobby's name on it.

In preparation for the draft, Bobby was invited to visit several NBA teams that were considering him as their No. 1 pick. He went to Orlando, Detroit, Sacramento, Denver, and Milwaukee. Then, at the last minute, the Los Angeles Lakers asked him to go out there.

Now it was the moment of truth. We arrived in Auburn Hills—Bobby, Chris, Melissa, our friend Bob Hahner, and me—on the day before the draft and the time just dragged until 7:00 P.M. draft day. We were all so nervous.

To pass the time on draft day, Chris and Bobby played gin rummy, which is a game-day ritual for them and probably one of the reasons Duke lost to California on Black Saturday. Chris wasn't there to play gin rummy with Bobby.

Another reason is my lucky tan pants weren't there, either. I have worn these lucky pants for years at every important game for St. Anthony and for Bobby and Danny, and the pants had never failed me. The pants were undefeated in Bobby's sophomore year in college, but they only work if someone's fanny is in them and they are at the site of the game. So it wouldn't have mattered if I had them on when I was watching Duke vs. California and Seton Hall vs. Western Kentucky on television.

I could have given the pants to somebody to wear at those games, but they disappeared a few weeks earlier. I don't know how we were able to win at St. Anthony without the pants. But I'm sure their absence hurt Duke and Seton Hall. The pants resurfaced the other day and I wore them to the draft for luck.

I study the draft very closely and I talked to a lot of other people who know what's going on, and the consensus was that Bobby would be the No. 7 pick and would go to the Sacramento Kings. But you never know.

There were rumors flying around that the New York Knickerbockers were trying to work out a deal to get Bobby, that the Boston Celtics were interested, and that the Los Angeles Lakers wanted him. So we were on pins and needles waiting to see what would happen.

All of the players projected to be first rounders were invited to attend the draft and to bring family and friends with them. We all sat at these large round tables backstage from where the draft was being conducted, in what was called "the green room."

The first pick belonged to the Orlando Magic and they selected Chris Webber of Michigan, who was coming out after his sophomore year. Webber, remember, is the guy who was doing all that trash-talking after Duke beat Michigan for the NCAA championship in 1992, and again this season.

After NBA Commissioner David Stern called out Webber's name, Chris got up and headed out to the podium. As he passed our table, he stopped and extended his hand to Bobby and said, "I'm glad I won't have to be seeing so much of you anymore."

It was a nice touch, a kind of bury-the-hatchet gesture between two young men who are about to be NBA pros.

We waited nervously as the draft proceeded. The Philadelphia 76ers, picking second, chose seven-foot, six-inch Shawn Bradley of Brigham Young. Golden State, picking third, took Anfernee Hardaway of Memphis State, and then Commissioner Stern announced a trade. The Magic and Warriors were swapping picks with the Warriors throwing in three future No. 1s in the deal. So, the wheeling and dealing was starting already.

The Dallas Mavericks took Jamal Mashburn of Kentucky with the fourth pick. Minnesota, drafting fifth, selected J.R. Rider of UNLV. Washington, with the sixth pick, chose Calbert Cheaney.

So far the draft was going as predicted. Now, the Sacramento Kings were up and my heart was pounding in my chest. The five minutes between selections seemed like an eternity. Then Commissioner Stern was at the microphone and we heard him say:

"With the seventh pick in the 1993 NBA draft, the Sacramento Kings select Bobby Hurley of Duke."

We were going crazy at the table in the green room. Everybody hugging one another. Bobby hugged me, then he hugged Chris, then he hugged Melissa. Somebody put a Kings baseball cap on his head and he started out to the main part of the arena to shake hands with Commissioner Stern, then to be interviewed on national television.

Later, Bobby said he didn't remember a thing from the moment they called his name. He didn't remember going out onto the podium, didn't remember what he said on television, didn't even remember who interviewed him. It took him some time to get his bearings.

· · ·

Bobby: As soon as I heard the "B" coming out of David Stern's mouth, I knew it was me. It was hard to believe this was happening to me.

· · ·

There were almost 14,000 in the arena and when Bobby's name was called, the fans started to boo and they kept booing all the while until he left the podium. He was the only one booed all night. This is Michigan country, remember, and they weren't booing Bobby Hurley of the Sacramento Kings, or Bobby Hurley of St. Anthony or Bobby Hurley of Jersey City. They were booing Bobby Hurley of Duke because, as Doug Collins said on television, he had helped Duke beat Michigan so often. In a sense, it was the ultimate tribute to Bobby.

The excitement had hardly died down for us when it started all over. A few minutes later, David Stern was at the microphone again.

"With the thirteenth pick in the 1993 NBA draft, the Los Angeles Clippers select Terry Dehere of Seton Hall University."

Once again, we were on our feet at our table, applauding and going crazy. We were ecstatic for Terry. He was going to a great situation for him and, at No. 13, he was chosen earlier than most people had predicted.

As he passed our table, Terry came over and gave me a hug. He hugged Chris and he hugged Melissa. He didn't say a word. I don't think he could have talked. He had that glazed look in his eyes.

Later, on television, Terry said some nice things about St. Anthony and about me, for which I am grateful. But I wouldn't have expected anything else from a kid like Terry.

Bobby and Terry got together and congratulated one another and already started talking about meeting up during the season. They'll both be on the West Coast, both in the same division, and they'll be playing against each other quite a bit, these two kids who were teammates at St. Anthony.

Later in the draft, with the No. 18 pick, the Utah Jazz selected 7—2 Luther Wright, who came out of Seton Hall early. Luther spent his freshman year at St. Anthony, so we count him as one of ours, too, and I wonder if three kids who attended the same high school ever were all first round NBA draft picks in the same year.

The one disappointment was that Jerry Walker was not drafted, but nobody really expected him to be. It might not be so bad. Now, he's a free agent, eligible to sign with any team. He'll get invited to camp by a lot of teams and his agent can look around and find the best fit for him. I have enough confidence and faith in Jerry's desire, his work ethic, and his talent to believe that whatever camp he goes to, he'll impress enough people to win a job. Even if he doesn't, it's not a total loss. Europe is a very viable option. So, he'll make some money and after a year or two in Europe, I'm sure he'll end up in the NBA.

While the draft was on, many of our friends and relatives were in Rosie Radigan's in Jersey City, which is owned by our friend, Rich McKeever, and which was having a special draft night party. They had a telephone hookup from the draft and Bobby spoke to the crowd there and they auctioned off the first pair of ITZ shoes for $1,300, plus some other items, and all proceeds were donated to the Jersey City Boys Club.

When the draft ended, we went back to our hotel. The bar at the Hilton was named "Hurley's," so you know we had to end up there. We took Bobby's name card from our table in the green

191

room and Bobby signed it and presented it to the manager at Hurley's bar. Then we ordered a bottle of Dom Pérignon and everybody had a little champagne to celebrate. Then we tried to go to sleep, but we couldn't.

The next morning, Melissa and I left at 4:30 to come home. Bobby and Chris flew to Sacramento, where they held a press conference for Bobby. They treated him like royalty. They made it clear he wasn't coming in as just a player, he was coming in as an important player. Chris loved Sacramento, as Bobby told her she would. He liked it when he visited there a couple of weeks ago. He said it reminded him of Durham, a small town, which he has gotten used to and which he likes.

I think it's a perfect situation for him. This is a kid who's lived all 22 of his years on the East Coast. Now, he will get some added balance in his life. Sacramento is only an hour and a half from San Francisco and an hour and a half from Lake Tahoe, so he has an opportunity to see a part of the country he's never seen.

As for the basketball situation, it couldn't be better. Bobby's happiness is predicated on getting the opportunity to play, and he knows he's going to get that with the Kings. Their goal for next season is to make the playoffs. They have a young team and they sell out all their home games at the Arco Arena. So, Bobby knows he's going to play and he's going to be seen by large crowds. The rest is up to him.

I would have liked him with the Knicks or the Celtics, but that's for purely selfish reasons. I would have been able to see him play more often. The most important consideration is his happiness and he couldn't be happier.

Besides, I've already ordered my satellite dish.